25-60

D1292836

Toward a Technology for Humanizing Education

David N. Aspy, Ph.D.
Northeastern Louisiana University

Research Press Company
2612 North Mattis Avenue
Champaign, Illinois 61820

CIP
Library of Congress Cataloging in Publication Data

Aspy, David N   1930-
      Toward a technology for humanizing education.
      Includes bibliographical references.
         1. Interaction analysis in education. 2. Teaching.
I. Title.
LB1084.A74   371.3'028   72-4552

ISBN 0-87822-028-3

5/17/74 *Robert Tayler* 3.00

This book is dedicated to the memory of
Carl D. Tatum — Educator

*Carl made life choices possible for the many who knew him as
teacher, coach, principal, and professor.*

Foreword

Since his path-finding research in 1963 relating the affective dimensions of the classroom to student achievement, Dr. David N. Aspy has come to distinguish himself as one of the leading educators of our time. In the tradition of Dewey he has demonstrated a sincere concern for the frame of reference of the learner. In the tradition of Watson he has attempted to operationalize and implement effective educational programs flowing from the learner's frame of reference.

Now Dr. Aspy has summarized his extensive work over the last decade in this book, enabling schools to humanize the educational process, for the next decade must be different from the last if—not education—but the world is to survive. Education is the cornerstone of fully functioning nations as well as individuals. It is with the goal of fully functioning peoples that Dr. Aspy has written this text.

It is a simple, straightforward text—written for educators and administrators as well as teachers, by an educator with extensive experience in administration as well as in teaching. Dr. Aspy shares with the reader the concepts, procedures, and techniques which he has used to maximize learning in the classroom. In this context, he produces the results of the empirical research and the research tools which he utilizes both to search his theses as well as to train his teachers and students. His approach is that of the teacher trainer—discerning the effective ingredients of teaching and transmitting them as directly as possible where they make the most difference—with the front-line teacher and student.

After an introduction to humanism in education by Carl Tatum, Dr. Aspy divides his text functionally into analyses of interaction and cognitive processes and the facilitative dimensions of empathy, regard, and genuineness. His chapters on these topics are fully descriptive and generative of new ideas for classroom teaching. Dr. Aspy goes on to apply his approach to issues of student involvement and success promotion. His chapters on these topics provide us with new perspectives on these critical teaching areas. Finally, Dr. Aspy concludes by demonstrating educational applications on a large scale. Most important, he calls for a "national consortium" to unify the efforts of educators and their systems in re-ordering humanistic educational priorities.

The committed teacher will find this text a handy sourcebook for new and more effective approaches to classroom teaching. The progressive administrator will find new perspectives to facilitate the development of his own educational direction. The intelligent lay public—parents as well as professionals in other areas—will find the book fresh and stimulating. Many will say that this is the way that they want their children to be educated. Indeed, this is the way they wish they had been educated.

Ultimately, the issues of education—and of life—are not to be settled in stale and stolid texts and journals. They are to be settled by putting our technologies "on the line"—testing them on the "human battleground"—in the vital classroom situation, modifying them to facilitate the students' fullest growth—physical and emotional as well as intellectual—and implementing them on the grander and grander human scales that weigh human life most heavily.

In summary, Dr. Aspy has succeeded in introducing us to the teaching methods that make the education of the next generation more feasible than the last. His book is indeed a first step "toward a technology for humanizing education." Its author will go on to operationalize that technology more fully, for his commitment to the educational process is a part of his commitment to his own personal growth. And the growth of generations that follow will be in part a function of the degree to which he and others like him operationalize such a humanistic, educational technology.

Robert R. Carkhuff, Ph. D.
Director, Center for Human Relations
and Community Affairs
Professor of Psychology and Education
American International College

Contents

Introduction:
HUMANISM IN EDUCATION

Humanism, variously defined, has long been a part of man's approach to living and seeking meaning in life, but in the last decade or so there has been a resurgence of the concept in the thinking and writings of men in all walks of life. We hear it spoken of not only by the philosophers, but by the theologians, the natural scientists, the architects, industrialists, business men, laboring men, the baker, and the candlestick maker.

How has this developed? What is there about our times that brings out so much talk of humanism?

What is it all about? What implications does it have for education?

Perhaps we can agree on some of the possible answers to the first question. Many writers in the humanistic tradition have said that modern man is so caught up in the accelerating pace engendered by his scientific discoveries, technological advances, and burgeoning knowledge that he is increasingly alienated from himself and his fellow men.

What it is all about is that many individuals the world over are saying, surely there must be more to living than this rat race we are in. Long accepted traditional reasons for living are undermined. Cries of "God is dead!" may be shouts of defiance or they might be pleas for some new god to come to the rescue. . .for man must work out some relationship with the cosmos. There seems to be a definite spiritual need, but it does not negate man's need to come to terms with himself and with other men outside himself. The humanists, as I interpret them, are neither shouting nor pleading. They are saying that man must work out his own meaning, and that in every way possible, he must help or allow other men to work out theirs.

What implications does humanism have for education? I think it means that we must seek to bring the feeling part of man more on a par with the thinking part of man; the affective domain in psychology must assume as much importance as the cognitive domain.

All of my professional educational life I have heard quotes of surveys which showed that 75-80% of human beings fail in the work-a-day world because they cannot relate effectively with other people; yet the major part of our educational effort is directed toward improving instruction—how to teach students more math earlier, interesting ways to present new *and* old facts. (I heard one of today's outspoken youth exclaim, "Why, the professor keeps asking me questions that he already knows the answers to!" A bit disquieting, that!) We have bigger and better reading programs, and we are producing so many non-readers that we are creating jobs in school after school for remedial reading teachers. (And I am happy to say that many of the remedial reading teachers that I know are finding that their best results occur when they set aside the textbook for awhile and relate to the child as a human being.)

Time after time I have heard college students say, "Whew! If I can just get through this exam tomorrow, I hope I never see another _____ textbook!" What a tragic waste of human effort—for the professor as well as the student.

What are we teaching best in our schools? We are teaching students not to think for themselves, but to think as we tell them to think. We are teaching them to be dependent on us, not to be independent and responsible. We are encouraging them to be devious, to misrepresent, to lose trust in themselves, to be inauthentic. In the process of getting an education students are persuaded, cajoled, bribed, and threatened in so many covert and overt ways that it is a wonder that there is anything left of selfhood when they come out.

How can humanism change all of this? Is it a panacea? Humanism cannot change *all* of this and it is *not* a panacea. In fact, one of the attractions it has for me is that it does not offer beautiful outside-of-me solutions, but rather encourages me to seek my own solutions.

What can we do about the powerful forces in our society which tend to squelch deviation and difference?

We can re-examine our own attitudes toward other human beings, asking ourselves seriously, how am I really affected by this person who dresses in a different way or chooses to allow the hair growing from various parts of his body to be arranged in different patterns—or chooses not to arrange it at all, or allows his clothing to be cut in a different style or absence of style, or uses Right Guard or does not, or uses or does not use certain patterns of speech or words, or whose skin—through genetically determined pigmentation, effects of the sun,

2

or use of cosmetics—reflects the light in a certain way. If we really want to relate to other human beings, we move toward them as they are.

Psychology, borrowing from the more established sciences, bent its efforts toward studying man in order to predict and control his behavior—albeit for his own good. In this light, educators see themselves as the experimenters and the people out there, the students, as subjects. But no man wants to be a subject. He wants to be an experimenter. We are all in favor of reorganizing the power structure, but we all want to be on the *permanent* central committee. The humanists, as I see them, do not want to cut down on research. Man must continue to study man. But the humanists are saying that we should involve the erstwhile subjects in the planning and execution of the experimental design—take into account the self-report, the feedback, the feelings expressed by all participants. In this way, research could be more helpful to human beings in their search for meaningful living.

In our society psychology has become too much identified with the manipulators. Psychologists have helped automobile manufacturers learn how to lure unsuspecting human beings into show rooms by displaying long, sleek, shiny convertibles, realizing that while only a small percentage of the customers actually buy convertibles, all of us like to imagine ourselves racing down the highway with the wind in our faces. And once they have lured us inside, the expert salesman, steeped in psychology of selling—ways of appealing to man's fears, vanity, greed, lack of self-concept—has us as fair game. Now what are the psychologists doing to help the unsuspecting human being make his *own* choices? These are humanistic concerns.

Somehow, in our process of studying man from the outside, we see him as he *compares* with other men in height, in visual acuity, speed of foot, reaction time, ability to see relationships—an endless accumulation of normative data. We have learned that among a thousand randomly selected children of a certain age we can predict at what level varying percentages of their number will respond to certain imposed tasks. This is very beautiful and satisfying to the experimenter, and surely of some help in projecting plans for larger groups; but what does it do for each individual human being who, in his own unique way, makes up this fine curve of distribution? Somehow we have fallen victims to elitism. If we are physical education teachers, we show our disdain for the clumsy child or upbraid the fat child who cannot do even one pull-up. If we are history teachers, we show our warm personal regard for the student who masters all the significant dates and names of important people; all of us bask in the sunshine of our brilliant students. We give short shrift to the dullards, saying to them by implication—if not openly—buckle down and work harder so you can be like the intellectual stars. What can they do? As one little girl said, looking with all the innocent sincerity of the very young into the disapproving eyes of her teacher, "If you don't like me the way I am, why don't you change me?" Why not accept them as worthy, just as worthy as anybody, just as they are, instead of misrepresenting to them that they can read as well as any other child, or that they can run as fast? They know the truth about that, and they know it early. But rather, let us say—and be sure that we genuinely feel or are trying to feel—that it does not matter at the living, human feeling level whether or not they can jump or run or read at an arbitrary level of competence, but that it does matter to us that they are alive and trying to get as much meaningful living done as they possibly can.

Humanism, to me, is helping others to work on the ever present question of, "Who am I?" It is keeping aware and helping others to keep aware of the suffering and grief, the brutality and tragedy in the world, as well as the joy and happiness that is here. It is to keep in touch with our feelings, to know and acknowledge our fear, our anger, our sorrow, our despair as well as our joy, our happiness, our love, so that we not become so hardened to the message from our senses that we read unperturbed of the growing list of dead in Vietnam, or see pictures of bloated, starving children in Biafra and not close our minds to the horror of it; and so that we not be so withdrawn that we fail to hear the pure note in a bird's song or feel thankful with the parched grass as summer rain comes down, or look with joy on a loved one, or exult in the surge of life that we feel within us.

Carl D. Tatum
Summer, 1969
His final lecture
at the University of Florida

4

An Overview: 1
THE WHAT AND WHY OF HUMANIZING EDUCATION

In writing this book, a deliberate attempt was made to avoid unnecessary complexity. Therefore, our explanation of the reason for this work is quite simple. Our purpose is to try to help all people·of "good will" in their efforts to make our schools healthier places for people to live and grow. Contained within this simple statement are several basic assumptions with which this book attempts to deal: (1) The first assumption is that schooling (and/or learning) is a process which occurs between individuals and it can be enhanced or diminished in effectiveness according to the degree of interpersonal facilitation with which it is carried out. (2) The second assumption is that all human beings—not just children—are engaged in a developmental process throughout life and can therefore benefit from a healthier interpersonal environment. (3) The third assumption is that interpersonal facilitation *can* be enhanced—in other words, it *is* possible for people to *learn* to be more understanding and caring for others.

The third assumption is considered to be a crucial one because efforts directed toward improving human relations are particularly important at this point in time—today the world's challenging frontier is that of helping people live together in mutual facilitation. For example, one writer estimates that in the near future more than 80% of the adult working population will be engaged in service-type occupations which will require competence in varying degrees of human relations behaviors and attitudes.[1] The headlines of almost any day's newspaper will supply further examples of the need for increased competency in healthy human relations. Thus, schools, as one of the chief sources of education for our citizens, should be involved in helping to enhance interpersonal functioning.

The foregoing words by themselves add nothing to what has already been said many times, because education has lacked neither humane

5

rhetoric nor men and women of good will. What it *has* lacked has been a technology to deal with the specific, "nitty gritty" problems encountered by schools in their attempts to help people become more effective in facilitating positive human growth and development. This book is addressed to those problems and provides a technology which can be applied to a school situation to assess processes of human interaction. Such assessments make it possible to train for improvement in interpersonal facilitation as well as to carry out research into basic classroom processes. The procedures included in this book were selected because they are "practical" in the sense that they have been employed successfully both by entire schools and by individual teachers. In other words, there is evidence to support the contention that these programs can and do work.

The Audience

The audience for this book consists of two large, but distinct, groups within the field of education. Although educators of today have so many functions and titles that classifying them is difficult, it is possible to distinguish these two large categories: (1) those directly or indirectly involved in classroom instruction, i.e., teachers, supervisors, and school administrators, and (2) those concerned primarily with research into classroom instruction. Obviously, there are innumerable exceptions to these divisions, but they can serve as workable groupings.

The differences in the concerns of the two groups come, of course, from the necessities of their respective situations. The instructional person needs an immediate measure which can give her clues to the action she should take. She is not so much concerned with getting an absolute level of correctness in her measurement of past or present behavior as she is with getting a quick indication of needed direction. She knows that the measure does not have to be too precise because she is constantly making adjustments in the action situation. The researcher, however, does not have continual access to the action situation. He reaches in, takes a slice of the action, and withdraws with it to his "laboratory" for detailed study of the relationships within or between samples. The meaningfulness of the generalizations he can draw from his study depends on the precision of the measurements he is able to take within each sample.

Thus, there are two levels of concern—one based on the need for immediacy, and the other on the need for more refined assessment. This book addresses both levels by presenting a technology appropriate for both and it is hoped that this can provide a communication vehicle between instructional people and researchers. These areas of concern have long remained mutually exclusive, and each has often failed to incorporate the insights of the other in its work. The classroom teacher tends to refer to the researcher as impractical, while the latter calls teachers uninformed about his work. Probably both are partially correct, but the procedures suggested in this book can close the gap by making each effort more relevant to the other.

The technology presented here reconciles the communication problem and the divergent needs of the two groups by presenting parallel versions of each measuring instrument. One version is designed to provide simple, immediate feedback about each of the processes being assessed. These measurements are referred to as in-service training scales. The other version, employing research scales, provides more precise measurements of each of the processes. This does not imply that a non-researcher should not use the research scales, but rather that the research scales require considerable time both to master and to apply. Training is helpful in the use of any of the scales, but if it is not available, the sincere, sensitive educator is encouraged to proceed with them as he would with any other professional procedure.

Procedures will be delineated for in-service training and research programs, and detailed examples of both will be given. The procedures presented in this book make it possible for a broad spectrum of workers and concerns to be brought together to promote more effective interpersonal relationships in our schools.

Process: A Preferred Criterion

There are many models for describing the classroom interaction, but, since we live in a technological society, an industrial model is likely to be a communicative vehicle. Thus, we can talk about three stages of production: (1) *input*, (2) *process*, and (3) *outcome*. Applying this notion to education, these stages might be phrased as three questions: (1) Where did we start? (2) What did we do? (3) Where did we finish? We currently spend a lot of time and money on things like achievement tests, IQ tests, cumulative records, attendance records, etc., which, in our industrial model, are either input or outcome measures. That is, they tell us where we started or what resulted from our process. Of course, these are important things to know; however, until recently, the day-by-day *process* has eluded us because we simply did not have the devices to examine it.

The kind of process referred to here is *not* the kind we obtain from statements like, "We're using the core curriculum," or "We're doing precision teaching." These are *not* processes. They are input intentions in the sense that they state the framework for what we would like to do. In our frame of reference, process involves the actual interpersonal interaction that occurs during the school day.

Why Is Process Important?
Process represents the reality of school. It tells us what actually happens instead of what we wish would happen. Reality, after all, is the only source of effective change, and looking at process (what we do) allows us to give ourselves *frequent* feedback about our classroom performance. Where else do we get feedback? Well, if we look to the results of standard achievement tests to assess our teaching, we usually will have a long wait, for these tests are often not given every year. Moreover, the results are subject to many debatable interpretations. Or, let us suppose we wait for supervisory reports. These often tell us if the supervisor likes the way we teach, and perhaps, all of this has some value. However, the maximum source of growth in teaching quite probably results from (1) a teacher's own knowledge of her own teaching process, and (2) an availability of resources to help her to improve whatever skills and knowledge she desires to improve.

This means that if she can examine her classroom processes, the teacher can devise her own in-service training program as the year progresses. She does not have to wait for test results or supervisory evaluations. In fact, when she is truly exploring her own classroom processes and discovering more effective levels of behavior, she will go beyond minimal professional levels. Also, she and the students will not have to spend a non-productive year wondering what is wrong. The processes of education can be discerned and altered as often as necessary, and to a great degree, outcome depends upon process.

Structure of the Book

There are three relatively new technologies which can provide data for investigating the humaneness of the interpersonal processes in a classroom, and these will be discussed in subsequent chapters. *First* Chapter 2 presents interaction analysis procedures which describe quantitatively the verbal components of a classroom interaction. That is, basically they tell us two things, (1) how frequently a specific verbal behavior occurs, and (2) the sequence of verbal behavior, or "what led to what." Since the interaction analysis procedure developed by Ned Flanders is easy to use and can be readily applied to classroom verbal interactions, this is the one which was selected for discussion.[2] However, there are many interaction analysis procedures available for use.

The *second* technology (discussed in Chapter 3) was developed by Benjamin Bloom to delineate seven types of cognitive functioning in a classroom. He called his scale Bloom's Taxonomy of Educational Objectives,[3] and Metfessel, et al., modified it to identify behavioral objectives for schools.[4] In turn, their procedure has been applied to assessments of the kinds of cognitive functioning of a classroom interaction. Thus, it is now possible to evaluate a specific classroom interaction in terms of the type of cognitive activity of (a) the teacher, (b) the student, and (c) the interaction between them. This means that we can determine the dynamic relationships between various kinds of cognitive activity.

The *third* technology is related to the assessment of levels of specific interpersonal conditions which determine whether an interaction is facilitating or retarding. Carl Rogers postulated that there are three critical dimensions of an interpersonal relationship, (1) Empathy, (2) Congruence, and (3) Unconditional Positive Regard;[5] and Carkhuff[6] modified and extended these dimensions and operationalized them in scales which could assess the levels of these conditions in psychotherapeutic interviews. He found that high levels of the conditions were related to client improvement, while low levels were associated with deterioration. These same scales were applied to classroom teaching by Aspy[7] who found them significantly and positively related to student achievement. Thus, there are specific interpersonal dimensions of the classroom interaction which can be described and assessed. Since each of these interpersonal conditions has been researched thoroughly, a chapter is devoted to each of them (Chapter 4—Empathy, Chapter 5—Congruence, and Chapter 6—Positive Regard).

Interpersonal relationships can also be assessed in terms of even more global dimensions, i.e., student involvement and the teacher's promotion of her students' success in achieving their goals. Scales for these measures are presented in Chapters 7 and 8. Both of these aspects of the classroom interaction have been found to be related to child-centered behavior, but the greatest value of these global dimensions is their common-sense communication to teachers. In other words, they are good starting points for training for assessments of the interpersonal relationship in a classroom quite probably because they were devised primarily by classroom teachers.

The scales and procedures presented in this book are (1) Flanders' Interaction Analysis, (2) Metfessel's, et al., Instrumentation of Bloom's Taxonomy of Educational Objectives, (3) Aspy's Scales for in-service training for facilitating interpersonal conditions, and (4) Carkhuff's

Scales for research assessment of facilitative interpersonal conditions. Each of the scales has been applied successfully to studies of classroom interaction.

The Procedures for Applying Instruments

Each of the instruments mentioned above may be applied to the verbal (audio) components of a classroom interaction. Since audio tape recording is relatively convenient and inexpensive, it is a feasible vehicle for preserving the classroom interaction for later assessment. For *research* purposes, the procedure employed most frequently in the past is composed of the following two steps:

1. Teachers tape record one hour of their "normal" classroom procedure.
2. The tapes are evaluated by three trained raters who apply a scale to four three-minute segments of the total hour. These usually are selected to represent samples of the teacher's performance throughout the hour. The teacher's total score is the mean of all the ratings by all the independent raters.

In-service training use of the scales has been somewhat less precise because the problems and needs in this situation are usually different from those of the research situation. The following procedure has been employed for in-service use:

1. A representative of the local school system is trained to use the scales, or

   A group of teachers is trained locally to use the scales.
2. The local school devises a plan for using the scales.
3. Each of the local participants audio tape records one hour of his classroom teaching and either sends it to be evaluated by experienced raters or evaluates it himself.
4. The teachers and/or system use the results of the scales for their own in-service training.

Since a teacher's time is limited, some arrangement for other people to do the rating may facilitate a teacher's use of this procedure. In a sense, this means using these reports just as a physician would use laboratory results to alter his treatment of patients. It should be remembered that these scales are technologies related to teaching and may contribute to effectiveness. They do not guarantee it.

10

Design of the Chapters

Each succeeding chapter will deal with a single scale for assessment of classroom interaction. At the outset of each chapter, the dimension with which it deals is defined and some of the relevant literature is presented. Next, there is an in-service training scale followed by a research scale for the measurement of each dimension. The final section of the chapter contains a study demonstrating how the scale for the dimension was used to answer a specific question in a "real-life" school setting.

Theoretical Basis

Self

This book is developed around the conception that each person is a self, as discussed in the writings of Combs, Maslow, Rogers, and Kelley.[8] Therefore, the technology presented is consistent with at least two of the basic tenets of self theory. *First,* since each self is unique in some way, the technology is designed to allow each teacher to discover her own most effective teaching behaviors. The advantage in using these procedures is that the teacher can make systematic changes in her teaching behaviors if she chooses to do so. That is, she has specific feedback about her performance and she can determine if she wants to change her classroom behaviors and how the change has affected other aspects of the teaching-learning situation. In short, this decreases some of the guesswork in her teaching.

A *second* property of the self is that it functions as a totality in the sense that each behavior has a relationship to every other aspect of self. Thus, the procedures reported in this writing were designed to enhance the opportunity that feedback will be received in a facilitative atmosphere, which means that the teacher is allowed to investigate her teaching in the way that she feels is most constructive for her. She alone knows her total response to the situation, and given the opportunity, she will devise the best procedures for promoting her growth. The challenge to the effective trainer is to create a facilitative atmosphere for constructive teacher growth.

Perceptions Influence Behavior

A teacher's behavior is a function of her perception of the situation. Therefore, in order to optimize her effectiveness, a teacher must perceive the entire classroom situation including herself as it *really* is. The scales, then, are systematic procedures designed to help the teacher improve her teaching by helping her to perceive components of the classroom which she may have been ignoring or only partially grasping.

The procedures for using the scales have been designed to enhance the conditions which will help each teacher perceive effectively. Specifically, trainees should be free from threat, and a successful learning experience is the major goal of each training session.

Perception Is Selective

The self behaves in keeping with its perceptions, and it is important to understand that seeing is *not* perceiving. That is, it is false to assume that because something is providing us sensory input, we are perceiving it. In this sense, perception is selective. What is perceived—assigned meaning—is determined by the perceiver and not by the external context. (For example, this writer viewed a video tape recording of a sample of his teaching for the purpose of assessing it and his entire response was focused upon his own camera appearance.)

The training implication of selective perception is that trainees must be allowed to describe their assessments of their teaching in order for the trainer to understand what they are perceiving. In this way, training sessions are discussions rather than lectures.

Summary

This book is directed toward humanizing the processes of education by providing teachers and researchers with procedures designed to assess the (1) verbal interaction, (2) cognitive levels, and (3) levels of interpersonal functioning in a classroom situation.

The general point of view is that if our classrooms are to become more humane, we need means by which we can provide teachers systematic and specific training designed for that purpose. It is also held that training procedures and trainers should exemplify the humane characteristics we want teachers to possess. In a sense, it is a matter of "doing unto others what we would have them do unto others." We might call this modeling behavior; however, the old phrase "practice what you preach" probably sums it up for most of us.

1. McKenna, B. H. School staffing patterns and pupil interpersonal behavior: Implications for teacher education. Burlingame: California Teachers Association, 1967. P. 27.

2. Flanders, N. A. *Interaction analysis in the classroom—A manual for observers.* Michigan: University of Michigan, 1965. P. 7.

3. Bloom, B. S., (Ed.), Englehart, M.D., Furst, E. J., Hill, W. H., and Krathwohl, D. R. *A taxonomy of educational objectives: Handbook I, The cognitive domain.* New York: Longmans, Green, 1956.

4. Metfessel, N.S., Michael, W. B., and Kirsner, D. A. Instrumentation of Bloom's and Krathwohl's taxonomies for the writing of educational objectives. *Psychology in the Schools,* 1969, *7* (3), 227-231.

5. Rogers, C. R. The necessary and sufficient conditions of therapeutic personality change. *Journal of Consulting Psychology,* 1957, *22,* 95-110.

6. Carkhuff, R. R. *Helping and human relations: A primer for lay and professional helpers. Vol. I. Selection and training. Vol. II. Practice and research.* New York: Holt, Rinehart and Winston, 1969.

7. Aspy, D. N. The effect of teacher-offered conditions of empathy, positive regard, and congruence upon student achievement. *Florida Journal of Educational Research,* 1969, *11* (1), 39-48.

8. Combs, A. W. (Ed.) *Perceiving, behaving, becoming.* ASCD Yearbook, 1962, Washington, D.C.: Association for Supervision and Curriculum Development, 1962.

Interaction Analysis: 2
IN HUMANE CLASSROOMS
STUDENTS SHOULD BE HEARD

The first technique to be explored in our efforts to construct a technology which will enable us to assess and/or improve the levels of humaneness within classrooms is interaction analysis. For our purposes this approach has two distinct advantages. *First,* it is understood and used by teachers. *Second,* it illustrates rather clearly that in most classrooms children are seen and not heard. This insight is a firm foundation on which to build in-service training directed toward humanizing education.

The following article by Campbell and Barnes appeared in *Phi Delta Kappan* in June, 1969. It is an excellent discussion of Flander's Interaction Analysis and recent research related to this procedure.

Interaction Analysis——A Breakthrough?*

Since publication of the Coleman Report, the *Kappan* has published several articles which directly state that research has failed to uncover any superior teaching methodology at any grade level. To quote from Millard Clements' article of October, 1968, "In most schools, the method of instruction, type of teacher, or size of class makes no difference in test performance."[1]

To some extent this contention is true, because no all-encompassing methodology has been discovered. In fact, researchers in this area have long abandoned this fruitless search. It is now apparent that teaching is so amazingly complex that no simple method will ever be found. Instead, researchers have simply attempted to isolate one or more

---

*By James Reed Campbell and Cyrus W. Barnes in *Phi Delta Kappan: A Journal for the Promotion of Leadership in Education.* Ed. Stanley M. Elam, June, 1969, *50* (10).

productive micro-elements of the complex instructional process and, therefore, limit the number of variables to a manageable number which could be measured in some fashion.

The search for the various micro-elements has been under way in dozens of research centers throughout the country. To date, researchers have isolated about 600 promising micro-elements in the 26 observational systems developed on the cognitive, psychological, and social levels.

The Flanders interaction analysis observational system is the most thoroughly developed. This system has isolated the following 10 verbal micro-elements on the psychological-social level (see Table 1). These categories are each mutually exclusive, so that a researcher is able to select one or more categories every three seconds during a teacher's lesson. In practice, a trained observer is capable of coding as many as 1,000 responses during a 45-minute lesson. Once the coding has been completed, the total number of tallies and the percentage of time spent in each category are calculated.

To further reduce the data, the category totals may be added in numerous combinations in order to produce a wide variety of interaction ratios. The two most widely used ratios are determined as follows:

$$\frac{I}{D} = \frac{Indirect}{Direct} = \frac{\text{Sum totals for Categories 1 to 4}}{\text{Sum totals for Categories 5 to 7}}$$

$$\frac{i}{d} = \frac{Indirect}{Direct} = \frac{\text{Sum totals for Categories } 1-3}{\text{Sum totals for Categories 6 \& 7}}$$

Research to date, both at New York University and other centers, has established the fact that average teachers (referred to as "direct") have I/D ratios below .40 and i/d ratios of below 1.00, while a select segment of teachers (referred to as "indirect") have ratios which are .7 and 2.00, respectively. When an indirect teacher has an i/d ratio of better than 2.00, he is spending twice as much time in the use of indirect (i) rather than direct (d) categories; i.e.,

$$\frac{i}{d} = \frac{1000}{500} = 2$$

Likewise, a direct teacher spends greater amounts of time in direct rather than indirect categories; i.e.,

$$\frac{i}{d} = \frac{750}{1000} = .75$$

16

Table 1

TEACHER BEHAVIORS

INDIRECT

1. Teacher accepts student's feelings.
2. Teacher praises student.
3. Teacher accepts or uses student's ideas.
4. Teacher asks question.

DIRECT

5. Teacher lectures.
6. Teacher gives direction.
7. Teacher criticizes.

STUDENT BEHAVIORS

8. Predictable student response to teacher question.
9. Student-initiated response.

MISCELLANEOUS

10. Silence or confusion.[2]

Once the teacher's verbal behavior has been quantified into an interaction ratio (independent variable), then it is possible to determine the effect of such teacher's behavior on achievement and attitude development (dependent variable).

Let us briefly review some of the more productive research studies done on this basis. Flanders[3] conducted a study (1955-56) involving the classes of 34 eighth-grade social studies teachers. He did another (1957)[4] involving the class of 34 New Zealand elementary teachers. Both studies showed that classes of the indirect teachers had higher levels of attitude development (.01 level).

In 1960 Flanders[5] conducted another experiment involving 16 eighth-grade math teachers and 16 seventh-grade social studies teachers. It showed that both attitude development and achievement were significantly better for the classes of indirect teachers. During 1961-62 Flanders and Amidon[6] conducted a study involving 560 eighth-grade math and 480 seventh-grade social studies students, producing the same results with significantly higher achievement and attitude development for the indirect group.

In another study at this grade level, LaShier (1966)[7] found significantly higher achievement and attitude development for eighth-grade biology classes of indirect student teachers.

On the elementary level, Brown (1960)[8] showed higher achievement in arithmetic among elementary classes of under- and over-achievers for

17

pupil-centered classes. Nelson (1966),[9] in a language arts study, found that first graders' compositions were superior both quantitatively and qualitatively in terms of total verbal output and vocabulary for the indirect methodology. Beltar, Weber, and Amidon (1966),[10] in a study of 100 culturally deprived kindergarten pupils, showed that indirect teachers produced greater gains from their classes on achievement measures.

Soar (1967),[11] in a study of 16 classes of third-, fourth-, fifth-, and sixth-grade youngsters, found vocabulary growth greater for indirect groups in grades three, four, and five. Furst and Amidon (1967),[12] in a study of high- and low-achieving groups of elementary youngsters, found that the high groups tended to have more indirect than direct teachers.

Davidson (1968),[13] in a study of children from grades two to six, found that indirect teachers produced higher levels of critical "thinking." Powell (1968),[14] found that indirect classes showed higher scores on SRA achievement tests, but no significant difference in reading achievement. Weber (1968),[15] in a study of 180 third- and fourth-grade youngsters, found that the indirect classes had higher scores on verbal creativity.

Finally, Campbell (1968),[16] in a study of 10 general science teachers and their seventh-, eighth-, and ninth-grade classes, found that the indirect group was significantly better in terms of achievement (STEP Test, .001 level) and scientific attitude development (Scientific Curiosity, Cause and Effect, Suspended Judgment, .05 level).

It is thus apparent that the micro-elements involved in the indirect/direct ratios (indirectness) do affect achievement and attitude development in almost every subject area at almost every grade level from K-9.

Even though much of this research is very recent and generally unpublished, it is surprising that the educational community appears not to be aware of the contribution being made in this area. In spite of this notable progress, it should be quite clear that no claim is being made for the discovery of a universal panacea for the solution of all our methodology problems. On the contrary, several studies on grade levels 10 to 16 have been unable to isolate any productive micro-elements within the Flanders system. In the hope of discovering some positive relationship at these levels, researchers at New York University have recently completed two exploratory studies at the senior high level and another at the community college level. Furthermore, within the next two years various members of this research group will conduct a number of cognitive and affective exploratory studies at these levels in order to extend and enlarge preliminary findings.

The research to date seems to indicate that explicit methodologies exist at the elementary, junior, and senior high levels; therefore, it is probable that different ratios and combinations will turn out to be specifically productive for each grade level.

However, the isolation of several crucial affective micro-elements at the elementary and junior high level is one of the most productive achievements of educational research. Finally, after years of failure and discouragement, we have isolated the first of many micro-elements which will eventually be utilized in a quantified theory of instruction. As an example of what such quantification will bring, let us illustrate how the 10 Flanders micro-elements can be used in analyzing the following 10 seconds of dialogue:

Time (Seconds)		Code
1	Teacher asks a long question	4
5	Student answers (briefly)	8
	Teacher uses his own opinion at length	5
10		5

The coded sequence would be 4-4-8-5-5 with the following combinations: 4-4, 4-8, 5-5. The combinations are formed by pairing each category with its predecessor and then again with its antecedent. Thus the student's response (8) was caused by the preceding (4) and resulted in the teacher's giving his own opinion (5). One hundred such combinations are utilized in analyzing a teacher's lesson by placing the sequenced data into a 100-cell 10 x 10 matrix. Since the matrix utilizes sequenced data, it can be used to analyze, at any one of 100 points, the incident that caused the category to appear or the incident that immediately followed any coded response. In practice, if a teacher's class suffers from excessive confusion, we can now present a concrete analysis of the teacher's verbal qualities that are causing the confusion. Furthermore, an individual's matrix can be compared cell by cell, column by column, with those matrices derived from the researchers cited above. We can, therefore, compare on the affective level one teacher's lesson with hundreds of direct and indirect teachers on a national basis. By such an analysis we can further determine objectively both the strengths and weaknesses of the lesson and diagnostically outline affective verbal patterns which have proved successful to a vast number of teachers at the same level. The potential productivity of such analysis is presently being widely explored in pre-service practice teaching courses and in-service courses.

However, the 100-cell analysis is no simple matter for the observer to interpret fully, and it is even more difficult for the teacher to implement the constructive elements specified. The complexity of such an approach is clearly evident when one category is isolated with its two-combination pairs; i.e., 4-1, 4-2, 4-3, 4-4, 4-5, 4-6, 4-7, 4-8, 4-9, 4-10. Each one of these pairs may be considered a distinct teacher mechanism for asking a question, and the implementation of each may involve a separate set of verbal behaviors and psychological skills. To make matters more complex, the research we have performed to date indicates that these two-category combinations are too narrow and limited for classroom use. Instead, three- and four-category combinations are infinitely more productive in the analysis of instruction. To illustrate, let us limit our analysis to the question (4) category and simply depict the one hundred resulting combinations (refer to Table 2). Each one of these combinations may be a fruitful method of asking a question and may involve a further complexity of human skills. It is probably clear to the reader that the total number of three-category combinations for the 10 interacting micro-elements is 1,000 (a 100-cell matrix for each category). In practice, our research shows that most direct teachers show a surprisingly small number of different patterns, while the indirect teacher shows at least a tenfold superiority in his variety of combinations. However, little research has been performed on these micro-combinations; therefore, in the summer of this year the N.Y.U. research staff will attempt to study several of these teaching patterns in the Allen-Gage teach-reteach micro-teaching technique by video-taping teachers as they isolate one or more of these elements. Perhaps combinations of four or five categories will result in providing the most fruitful approach. Although the resulting complexity would involve the astounding number of 100,000 combinations, a much smaller number will doubtlessly turn out to be productive. The implications of this research are twofold:

First, objective analysis of the teaching process: At long last we can approach objective evaluation instead of the wide-spread subjective process now in vogue. We can now give a teacher something definite, both in the form of a diagnosis and subsequent prognosis to utilize in improving his teaching, and perhaps we can move away from the hopelessly vague folklore which has come to be known as education.

In the twenty-first century, when the historians of education speak of the present era of supervision, they will doubtless be astounded that any individual could observe a class, see so much, understand so little, and produce a crisp evaluation of the teacher, the process, and the content in so short a time. The resulting superficiality has become apparent both to teachers and their militant spokesmen.

Second, theory of instruction: It is probably clear that the complexity and fruitfulness of even 10 micro-elements is almost without limit. In the years to come, many of these combinations will be eliminated while others will turn out to be highly productive. It must be further emphasized that our entire discussion has been limited to only 10 micro-elements on the psychological-social level, and the final process of teaching may involve hundreds or even thousands of distinct non-overlapping micro-elements. Out of the 600 elements now under investigation, at least 200 are nonrecurring, and the number of entirely distinct elements will continue to grow. Certainly, the resulting complexity of even a 100-category system with two interacting combinations would involve 10,000 different patterns, while combinations of three elements would involve well beyond a million distinct teaching patterns.

It is probably clear why the old global, head-on, all-inclusive methodology studies of the past have failed to uncover a single, simple method which could be used in K-16 to solve all our educational problems. In fact, such an approach seems to have been a preposterous undertaking in view of our present knowledge of the complexity involved.

Table 2 Category 4—Teacher Asks Question

(Three-Category Combinations)

Category	1	2	3	4	5	6	7	8	9	10
1	411	412	413	414	415	416	417	418	419	4110
2	421	422	423	424	425	426	427	428	429	4210
3	431	432	433	434	435	436	437	438	439	4310
4	441	442	443	444	445	446	447	448	449	4410
5	451	452	453	454	455	456	457	458	459	4510
6	461	462	463	464	465	466	467	468	469	4610
7	471	472	473	474	475	476	477	478	479	4710
8	481	482	483	484	485	486	487	488	489	4810
9	491	492	493	494	495	496	497	498	499	4910
10	4101	4102	4103	4104	4105	4106	4107	4108	4109	41010

What will education be like with such a complex system? What will be the role of the teacher in view of such complexity? Perhaps teachers will rely heavily on specific combinations analyzed and tailored for individual groups by the computer. Perhaps teachers will specialize in one segment of the teaching process, and by the means of teams present material to a given group of students. Perhaps the computer will be the only instrument capable of handling such a theory of instruction. Whatever the final result, this quantification process will radically change teaching as we know it today.

Describing Classroom Verbal Interaction

Using the In-Service Training Scale

This in-service training scale is designed for three purposes: (1) to introduce educators to the procedures of systematic examination of classroom processes, (2) to introduce evidence to educators that, generally speaking, *teachers talk too much in their classrooms,* and (3) to prepare educators for the use of Flander's Interaction Analysis.

The in-service scale is presented in two levels, Stage I and Stage II. Stage I serves as a simple introduction to the systematic analysis of verbal interaction, for it requires the trainee to make only a *quantitative* decision about the interaction while following the general process (listen, decide, record) involved in more sophisticated analysis. Once teachers are comfortable with the procedure involved in Stage I, the additional *qualitative* decisions required for analysis at Stage II are easily mastered. In this way, the trainees are prepared to move to Flander's Interaction Analysis.

In order to make the transition between scales as trouble-free as possible, the in-service scale (both stages) uses the same general directions for the observer as those given for Flander's Interaction Analysis. They are:

1. Listen to three seconds of classroom verbal interaction.
2. Decide which category best describes the interaction during that three seconds.
3. Record the number of the category.

These recorded numbers provide a map of the flow of verbal interaction in a classroom. However, the main concept—that most of the verbal output in most classrooms is from teachers—is communicated quite adequately by totaling the number of marks in each category. Also, since precision of ratings is not a major goal with the in-service scales, usually no attempt is made to achieve a particular level of agreement.

In-Service Training Scale: Classroom Verbal Interaction

Stage 1	Category	Speaker
	1	Teacher
	2	Student
	3	Several people simultaneously
	4	Silence

Stage 2	Category	Description of Behavior
	1	*Teacher* who seems to be talking *at* the students, i.e., lecturing or "making a speech."
	2	*Teacher* who seems to be talking *with* the students, i.e., normal conversation or responding to students' questions.
	3	*Student* who seems to be talking *at* other people, i.e., lecturing or "making a speech."
	4	*Student* who seems to be talking *with* other people, i.e., normal conversation.
	5	*Several people simultaneously,* most or all of whom seem to be interested in the topic of discussion.
	6	*Several people simultaneously,* few, if any, of whom seem involved in the same topic of discussion.
	7	*Silence.*

Using Flanders' Interaction Analysis

There seems to be an element of serendipity in the almost simultaneous emergence of interaction analysis and audio tape recordings. The tapes are particularly suitable as an economical means of "freezing" verbal interaction for subsequent investigation, while analysis such as that delineated by Flanders provides a specific procedure for carrying out the investigation. Of course, the analysis can also be applied to "live" classroom process.

The procedures for interaction analysis are pretty straightforward and rather easily learned. The important concept is that the analysis is directed toward the verbal elements of the classroom interaction. The observer follows these basic steps:

1. Listen to three seconds of classroom verbal interaction.
2. Decide which category best describes the interaction during that three-second period.
3. Record the number of the category.

This procedure allows for a continuing record of the classroom interaction. The observer listens to the next three seconds while he is recording the number for the preceding period. Thus, as he listens and records the numbers in sequence, he provides a dynamic record of the verbal interactions in a classroom.

Since Flanders' Interaction Analysis can be used for both in-service training and research, it is important to discuss some aspects of its use which are specific to the training process. As with all instruments for in-service training, precision of rating is less important than the communication of an understanding which leads to more effective teaching. Therefore, inter-rater reliability is usually ignored in this context. The trainer may use a variety of methods in introducing and teaching the technique, but we have found the following sequence helpful:

1. The trainees learn to use the scale by applying it to standardized tapes of classroom interaction.
2. The trainees are asked to volunteer to tape record some of their teaching and share it with a small group (4-5) of their colleagues. No one is forced to tape record his class.

The training sessions usually consist of rating segments (three minutes) from a variety of tapes rather than entire tapes.

Teacher Talk	Indirect Influence	1. *Accepts Feelings:* Accepts and clarifies the feeling tone of the students in a non-threatening manner. Feelings may be positive or negative. Predicting or recalling feelings are included.
		2. *Praises or Encourages:* Praises or encourages student action or behavior. Jokes that release tension, not at the expense of another individual, nodding head or saying, "um hum" or "go on" are included.
		3. *Accepts or Uses Ideas of Students:* Clarifying, building, or developing ideas suggested by a student. As teacher brings more of his own ideas into play, shift to Category 5.
		4. *Asks Questions:* Asking a question about content or procedure with the intent that a student answer.
	Direct Influence	5. *Lecturing:* Giving facts or opinions about content or procedure; expressing his own ideas, asking rhetorical questions.
		6. *Giving Directions:* Directions, commands, or orders to which a student is expected to comply.
		7. *Criticizing or Justifying Authority:* Statements intended to change student behavior from nonacceptable to acceptable pattern; severe criticism of student's behavior; statements why the teacher is doing what he is doing; extreme self-reference.
Student Talk		8. *Student Talk–Response:* Talk by students in response to teacher. Teacher initiates the contact or solicits student statement.
		9. *Student Talk–Initiation:* Talk by students which they initiate. If "calling on" student is only to indicate who may talk next, observer must decide whether student wanted to talk. If he did, use this category.
		10. *Silence or Confusion:* Pauses, short periods of silence, and periods of confusion in which communication cannot be understood by the observer.

An Application of Flanders' Interaction Analysis*

The task of humanizing our classrooms, like other fundamental changes in education, is difficult indeed. However, an encouraging development has appeared, and its widespread applicability to education seems to provide a new and potentially powerful device for the change process. This new development is a procedure that involves three basic components: (1) audio tape recording classroom teaching, (2) evaluating the recordings (by trained raters), and (3) communicating the ratings to the teachers who made the recordings. The raters *and* teachers should have been trained previously to apply scales designed to assess various dimensions of a classroom interaction. The rating procedure used is a modification of one developed for investigation of psychotherapy by Carl Rogers and his co-workers and subsequently extended to other interpersonal situations by such researchers as Carkhuff.

One specific application of this procedure was made in a study involving 32 secondary English teachers who were enrolled in a six-week summer workshop. The general emphasis of the workshop was directed toward helping the teachers become more student-centered in their classroom practices. The major thrust was to create a facilitative climate within which trainees could learn specific procedures for improving the humaneness of their classroom interaction.

Procedure

Selecting supervisory personnel. The first step in creating a facilitative climate for the teacher-participants involved the painstaking screening of the supervisors, principals, and other administrative workers who would be involved in the workshop. These personnel were selected on the basis of two criteria: (1) professional competence, and (2) ability to provide high levels of empathy, congruence, and positive regard in a human interaction. Judgments as to competency were based on evaluations supplied by co-workers, while assessments of levels of interpersonal functioning were made by three trained raters from tape recordings of interviews with teachers. Each supervising person selected for the program was judged fully competent and performed above minimal levels for facilitative interpersonal functioning—3.0, as determined by previous research.

---

*Abridged from: D. N. Aspy, The Relationship of the Trainer's Level of Interpersonal Functioning and Change in Teacher Behavior. *Educational Leadership Research Supplement,* 1971, *28.*

Use of A-V equipment. The second procedure involved instructing the trainees in the mechanics of both an audio and video tape recorder. The purpose of this procedure was not only to acquaint the trainees with the mechanics of those devices, but also to create a favorable relationship with the supervisory personnel whose services were available to the participants. The trainees were told that both the audio and video tape machines could be used by them at any time; however, they would never be required to use them.

Use of rating scales. The third phase of the program was directed toward familiarizing the participants with specific scales which can be used in the evaluation of audio tape recordings of classroom interactions. The scales were (1) Flanders' Interaction Analysis and (2) Carkhuff's Scales for Empathy, Congruence, and Positive Regard. Each of the scales was demonstrated by use of sample tapes of classroom teaching. The trainees demonstrated a high degree of agreement (above 80%) in their ratings of those tapes, and all of the supervising personnel reported from the follow-up small-group discussions that the participants seemed to have a sound grasp of the concepts underlying the scales as well as the procedures for applying them.

The trainers' levels of interpersonal functioning. The thirty-two trainees were divided into two groups for instruction in the use of the rating scales. The groups were matched for years of experience and sex (5 males and 11 females in each group), and each group received 15 hours of training with the scales. All the training sessions for each group were led by the same trainer, and each session was tape recorded and assessed for the trainers' levels of empathy, congruence, and positive regard. These assessments were completed blind by three experienced raters whose inter-rater correlations were above .75. The means of those ratings are listed in Table 1.

Since these ratings indicate that Trainer A was functioning above the minimal level of facilitative interpersonal conditions (3.0) while Trainer B was functioning below this point, it was possible to investigate the effect of each trainer's level of interpersonal functioning upon the trainees.

The trainees' levels of interpersonal functioning. To determine the trainees' levels of interpersonal functioning, two hours of audio tape recordings of their classroom teaching were evaluated by Flanders' Interaction Analysis and Carkhuff's Scales for Empathy, Congruence, and Positive Regard. The audio tape recordings were made during the

27

Table 1

	Trainer A	Trainer B
Empathy	4.1 *(3.9-4.3)	1.0 *(1.5-2.2)
Congruence	4.3 *(4.0-4.5)	1.6 *(1.4-1.7)
Positive Regard	4.5 *(4.3-5.0)	1.5 *(1.0-1.7)

*Range: Trainer's mean levels of functioning according to ratings obtained from Carkhuff's Scales. Level "1" corresponds to lowest levels, while level "5" corresponds to highest levels.

first and last week of the training program. Thus, it was possible to assess both entering levels of functioning and changes during the training period.

Results

A summary of the analyses of the trainees' audio tape recordings is listed in Table 2. The data indicates that the trainees of the "high" level trainer made significant changes ($p > .05$) in four categories of the Flanders' Interaction Analysis, while those of the "low" conditions trainer did not make significant change in any of the categories.

Conclusion

Attempts to humanize classrooms are differentially effective, and the recent developments of relatively inexpensive audio tape recording equipment combined with the procedures reviewed in this study may provide a potent device for enhancing that effect. This means that we can systematically investigate specific incidents in teaching and perhaps help teachers delineate the components of their most effective teaching.

This study supports a second assertion, namely, that the person who trains teachers must himself provide high levels of facilitative

Table 2

Relationship Between Change in Trainees' Performance and
Levels of Facilitative Conditions Provided by Trainers

Flanders' Interaction Analysis Categories		Mean of Percentages of Trainee's Behavior in Category					
		N = 16 Recipients of *high levels* of facilitative conditions			N = 16 Recipients of *low levels* of facilitative conditions		
		June	July	Change	June	July	Change
	1	0	0	0	1	1	0
Indirect	2	1	1	0	1	2	+1
Influence	3	7	19	+12*	7	16	+9
	4	17	10	-7	16	20	+4
Direct	5	23	7	-16*	25	19	-6
Influence	6	3	1	-2	7	1	-6
	7	2	0	-2	2	0	-2
Student Talk	8	25	12	-13*	20	24	+4
	9	13	42	+29**	14	11	-3
Silence or Confusion	10	7	6	-1	6	6	0

*Significant at .05 Level. **Significant at .01 Level.

interpersonal conditions. Of course, the small number of trainers involved in this study limits generalizations. However, the data is strongly supported by research from psychotherapy. The major significance of this study is that it demonstrates the kind of procedures which could be applied to a broad range of educational settings.

Finally, this study supports the contention that learning which takes place in a relatively humane atmosphere is more likely to be translated into practice than learning from an inhumane climate. Perhaps by using this procedure researchers may add to their findings that humaneness is important in the facilitation of constructive change in the human beings with whom we work.

1. Clements, M. Research and incantation: A comment. *Phi Delta Kappan,* October, 1968, p. 107.

2. Flanders, N. A. *Interaction analysis in the classroom–A manual for observers.* Michigan: University of Michigan, 1965. P. 7.

3. Flanders, N. A. *Teacher influence, pupil attitudes and achievement.* Washington, D. C.: U.S. Government Printing Office, 1965. Pp. 50-65.

4. *Ibid.,* pp. 53-65.

5. *Ibid.,* p. 114.

6. Amidon, E. and Flanders, N. A. The effect of direct and indirect teacher influence on dependent-prone students learning geometry. *Journal of Educational Psychology,* December, 1961.

7. LaShier, W. S. An analysis of certain aspects of the verbal behavior of student teachers of eighth-grade students participating in a BSCS laboratory block. *Dissertation Abstracts,* June, 1966, pp. 7, 168.

8. Brown, G. I. Which pupil to which classroom climate? *Elementary School Journal,* February, 1960.

9. Nelson, L. Teacher leadership: An empirical approach to analyzing teacher behavior in the classroom. *Journal of Teacher Education,* Winter, 1966, p. 425.

10. Belter, E. K., Weber, W. A., and Amidon, E. J. *Classroom Interaction Newsletter,* December, 1965, p. 9.

11. Soar, R. S. Pupil needs and teacher-pupil relationships: Experiences needed for comprehensive reading. In *Interaction analysis: Theory, research, and application.* Massachusetts: Addison-Wesley Publishing Co., 1967. Pp. 243-50.

12. Furst, N. and Amidon, E. J. Teacher-pupil interaction patterns in the elementary school. In *Interaction analysis: Theory, research, and application.* Massachusetts: Addison-Wesley Publishing Co., 1967. Pp. 167-75.

13. Davidson, R. L. The effects of an interaction analysis system on the development of critical reading in elementary school children. *Classroom Interaction Newsletter,* May, 1968, p. 13.

14. Powell, E. V. Teacher behavior and pupil achievement. *Classroom Interaction Newsletter,* May, 1968, p. 24.

15. Weber, W. A. Teacher behavior and pupil creativity. *Classroom Interaction Newsletter,* May, 1968, p. 34.

16. Campbell, J. R. Cognitive and affective process development and its relation to a teacher's interaction ratio. Unpublished doctoral thesis, New York University, 1968.

17. Flanders, *Interaction analysis in the classroom.*

Cognitive Processes: 3
IN HUMANE CLASSROOMS
STUDENTS SHOULD THINK

The inclusion of a chapter about cognitive processes might be a bit puzzling to the reader who expected this writing to concentrate solely upon the affective domain. However, the central notion out of which this book developed is that a truly humane classroom is one in which all of the highest abilities of a person are nurtured. Therefore, since cognition is perhaps man's highest evolutionary development, it is an integral concern of humane classrooms.

The public school is charged primarily with the responsibility for promoting the cognitive growth of its students. We commonly say that we try to make children smarter, and this notion is the center of a major controversy among educators. Specifically, the question revolves around the proper criterion for intelligence and how cognitive growth is promoted. To some educators students are brighter if they know a lot of facts; so they advocate fact-centered curricula and processes. Other educators maintain that cognitive ability involves not only facts but also processes or ways of applying intellectual capacity. Generally, this latter area is called thinking. As a result of this concept, they argue for curricula and processes which place emphasis upon both gathering facts and thinking. One of the best discussions of this basic issue was formulated by Bigge and Hunt in their fine book, *Psychological Foundations of Education.* Therefore, that discussion follows.

How Can Schools More Effectively
Promote Intelligence?*

Teaching-learning situations may be classified according to where they

*By Morris L. Bigge and Maurice P. Hunt, *Psychological foundations of education.* New York: Harper and Row, 1968.

fall on a continuum which ranges from "thoughtless" to "thoughtful" modes of operation. However, it is convenient to divide their total range into three broad classifications: memory level, understanding level, and reflection level. Memory level is most "thoughtless" and reflection level most "thoughtful." Products of both the understanding and the reflection level are understanding or insights plus increased ability of the learner to achieve further understanding or insights independently.

What Is Memory Level Learning and Teaching?

Memory level learning is that kind of learning which supposedly embraces committing factual materials to memory and nothing else. We all know how this can be done; it is possible for a person to memorize virtually any type of material, including that which seems quite nonsensical. The more meaningful the material to be learned, the easier it is to memorize. Furthermore, the more meaningful the learned material, the longer it tends to be retained. A collection of "nonsense" syllables might conceivably be remembered for a lifetime if a person had sufficient reason for retaining the information. However, when one develops a reason for retaining something, it is no longer nonsensical.

At first glance, rote-memory learning seems to exemplify a mental discipline or S-R associationistic theory of learning; either a substantive mind is trained or simple linkages are formed between stimuli and responses with no particular thought or purpose involved. But a cognitive-field psychologist denies that either is the case. Instead he insists that, if anything is learned at all, insight of a sort is always present. What characterizes rote learning, to a cognitive-field theorist, is that the insights acquired usually have no significant relationship to the material being studied. However, the learned material is patterned by the learner during the process of his learning it. Even "nonsense syllables," when learned, are not completely unpatterned.

Capacity to memorize and retain material probably bears no positive relationship to capacity for intelligent behavior. Geniuses are notoriously forgetful, although not usually in their areas of major interest. Conversely, a mentally defective person may be highly proficient in memorization. Polly was a 13-year-old girl with the mental capacity of an imbecile. She had a quite brilliant memory of the "shotgun" variety. That is, she memorized verbatim an overheard conversation or a radio newscast. After hearing it once, she could recite faultlessly the words of every popular song being broadcast at the time. Nevertheless, Polly's "thought power" was so impaired that, if asked to close an outside door of the house, she could not decide on which side of the door to stand to avoid shutting herself out.

Every experienced teacher can recall numerous students who developed a considerable capacity to memorize standard curricular materials in most or all school subjects. Such students usually make high marks. However, when they take a course with a teacher who employs problem-centered teaching, they may become extremely frustrated and do very poor work. Conversely, an experienced teacher also can recall students whose marks were spotty but who achieve magnificently once they got out of school. There is a fairly good chance that in such cases poor achievement in school is a rebellion against rote memorization.

Memory level teaching may, of course, contribute indirectly to intelligent behavior. If memorized facts become pertinent on an occasion when a problem requires solution, they contribute to useable background and hence to the effectiveness of problem solving. However, memorized facts usually contribute little to effective student growth. One reason is that, as already suggested, they tend to be forgotten quickly. Another is that a large proportion of the facts memorized in school are irrelevant to future thought needs. In summarizing the value of rote memory teaching we might even say that the best way to make sure that a student will not remember many facts is to place the whole emphasis upon teaching him facts.

It no longer is a matter for speculation that not much in the way of durable or useful results can be expected from memory level instruction. Its contribution to intelligent behavior is too unpredictable and undependable for us to set much store by it as a favored instructional procedure. Yet there is no reason to suppose that most teachers are dedicated to some other approach. No matter how much talk is raised against straight memory level instruction, there are numerous pressures placed on teachers to confine teaching to this level. Furthermore, many teachers may have no vision of anything different.

Despite all the legitimate criticisms we may make of rote memorization, it would be unrealistic to suppose that a teacher can always avoid it. In any ordinary school situation, there are occasions when even the most imaginative teacher will have no better approach than memory level teaching. This may occur on days when lack of time has prevented planning anything else. Or it may happen when the teacher does not know how else to handle the material to be covered.

One might ask, "Can the fundamental skills, such as spelling, be taught otherwise than through a process of straight memorization, using drill procedures?" Generally speaking, they *can* be taught more efficiently through other procedures. However, much more study will be required to develop procedures for teaching all the fundamental skill subjects in ways which will free us entirely from rote memorization.

What Is Understanding Level Learning and Teaching?

Although a careful analysis of the nature of understanding . . . [is not possible here], our purposes require a short definition [now]. A common definition of understanding is "seeing the use to which something may be put." For example, if Johnny knows a use to which he can put his knowledge that Columbus sailed to the West Indies in 1492, we may say that he "understands" the data.

A more sophisticated definition retains the idea of purposeful use but includes another element: the relationship between the general and the particular. A fact or group of facts is said to be understood if their evidential relationship to a principle is seen. That is, if a student sees that a particular fact either supports or casts doubt on some principle, he understands the fact. Likewise, they are operating on the same level when they teach theories in physics, chemistry, or football. (A rule or principle, by definition, is a theoretical statement.) A clear contrast may be drawn between understanding level and memory level teaching. Whereas memory level teaching tends to ignore principles, or at best handles them on such a superficial level that they have no meaning, understanding level teaching, if successful, gives students knowledge of the principles by which facts are related to one another, as well as of the facts themselves. If a person really understands a principle or a generalization, he probably can (1) state it in his own words, (2) give examples of it, (3) recognize it in various guises and circumstances, (4) see relationships between it and other principles or generalizations, (5) use it in diverse situations, (6) anticipate the consequences of its application, and (7) state an opposite principle.

From the standpoint of educational psychologists, understanding level is much to be preferred over memory level teaching. They would argue that much of the inefficiency in education, which research has exposed, stems from the way most school subjects are organized and presented. Subjects often remain meaningless to students, not because of students' intellectual deficiencies, but because human mentalities work in such a way that the subjects as organized and taught have little meaning for them.

Understanding level teaching gives students a tool for more intelligent behavior. It equips them with generalized insights which can be applied in problematic situations both in and outside school. It provides them with a mental kit of rules. If the rules learned are the best that are known at the time by people in a position to have expert knowledge, students have at least gained something from education.

By this time readers may have sensed that there is still something lacking. Understanding level teaching, if it remains merely that, casts the student as a passive and the teacher as an active agent. The teacher tells, the student listens or the teacher stimulates and the student responds. Understanding level teaching may be highly uncritical and authoritarian. Furthermore, the principles taught by the teacher may be wrong—and sometimes are. Consequently, understanding level teaching may lead to more intelligent behavior on the part of a student, but it does not carry with it the quality of experience needed to enhance intelligence to its fullest potential.

Measuring Cognitive Behavior in a Classroom

Using the In-Service Training Scale

The in-service training scale for the measurement of cognitive behavior in a classroom has two primary purposes: (1) to demonstrate that using facts (thinking) is appropriate classroom behavior, and (2) to demonstrate that students are sources of cognitive activity. Both of these concepts are important at this time, because of two facts: (1) most classroom activity is limited to memory and recall, and (2) teachers tend to dominate the cognitive activity in a classroom.

The training sessions usually consist of the following steps:

1. The trainer makes a didactic explanation of cognitive process and the scale.
2. The group listens to a standard audio tape recording of classroom teaching and rates the cognitive level of *each* verbal response during a three-minute segment. The ratings are discussed and the trainer continues this procedure until the group seems proficient in the use of the scales.
3. The group, if large, is divided into small groups (4 or 5) and volunteers present recordings of their teaching for the group to rate. This procedure is repeated as long as it seems productive for the group.

Since the central focus of the in-service training scale is communication rather than precision, the training sessions are not primarily concerned with statistical reliability. The trainer concentrates upon the trainees' apparent understanding of cognitive processes and the use of the scale.

In-Service Training Scale: Cognitive Behavior in a Classroom

Behaver	Category of Behavior

Teacher

1. Demonstrates knowledge of a fact.
2. Asks someone else to demonstrate knowledge of a fact.
3. Uses a fact.
   Examples: (a) to solve a problem,
   (b) to analyze a situation.
4. Asks students to use a fact.
   Examples: (a) to solve a problem,
   (b) to analyze a situation.

Student

5. Demonstrates knowledge of a fact.
6. Asks someone else to demonstrate knowledge of a fact.
7. Uses a fact.
   Examples: (a) to solve a problem,
   (b) to analyze a situation.
8. Asks someone else to use a fact.
   Examples: (a) to solve a problem,
   (b) to analyze a situation.

Using the Metfessel, Michael, and Kirsner Scale

The Metfessel, Michael, and Kirsner Instrumentation of the Taxonomy of Educational Objectives (Cognitive Domain) was designed primarily for the formulation of educational objectives and allows for detailed examination of the level of cognitive processes. Therefore, when it is applied to a classroom interaction, it is essential that the interaction be audio or video tape recorded, permitting the rater to control the speed of the verbal output.

For research purposes three raters evaluate four three-minute segments from one hour of classroom teaching. The raters, working independently, assign a rating to each verbal output during the selected segments. (An inter-rater reliability of .85 is achieved by experienced raters, and, in fact, this level of agreement is necessary for research purposes.) A copy of the scale and the following tally sheet is provided each rater for each tape recording to be assessed.

Instrumentation of the Taxonomy of Educational Objectives: Cognitive Domain

Taxonomy Classification	Key Words	
	Examples of Infinitives	Examples of Direct Objects
1.00 Knowledge		
1.10 Knowledge of Specifics		
1.11 Knowledge of Terminology	to define, to distinguish, to acquire, to identify, to recall, to recognize	vocabulary terms, terminology, meaning(s), definitions, referents, elements
1.12 Knowledge of Specific Facts	to recall, to recognize, to acquire, to identify	facts, factual information (sources, names, dates, events, persons, places, time periods), properties, examples, phenomena
1.20 Knowledge of Ways and Means of Dealing with Specifics		
1.21 Knowledge of Conventions	to recall, to identify, to recognize, to acquire	form(s), conventions, uses, usage, rules, ways, devices, symbols, representations, style(s), format(s)
1.22 Knowledge of Trends, Sequences	to recall, to recognize, to acquire, to identify	action(s), processes, movements, continuity, development(s), trend(s), sequence(s), causes, relationship(s), forces, influences
1.23 Knowledge of Classifications and Categories	to recall, to recognize, to acquire, to identify	area(s), type(s), feature(s), class(es), set(s), division(s), arrangement(s), classification(s), category/categories
1.24 Knowledge of Criteria	to recall, to recognize, to acquire, to identify	criteria, basics, elements
1.25 Knowledge of Methodology	to recall, to recognize, to acquire, to identify	methods, techniques, approaches, uses, procedures, treatments
1.30 Knowledge of the Universals and Abstractions in a Field		

Taxonomy Classification	Key Words	
	Examples of Infinitives	Examples of Direct Objects
1.31 Knowledge of Principles, Generalizations	to recall, to recognize, to acquire, to identify	principle(s), generalization(s), proposition(s), fundamental(s), laws, principal elements, implication(s)
1.32 Knowledge of Theories and Structures	to recall, to recognize, to acquire, to identify	theories, bases, interrelations, structure(s), organization(s), formulation(s)
2.00 Comprehension		
2.10 Translation	to translate, to transform, to give in own words, to illustrate, to prepare, to read, to represent, to change, to rephrase, to restate	meaning(s), sample(s), definitions, abstractions, representations, words, phrases
2.20 Interpretation	to interpret, to reorder, to rearrange, to differentiate, to distinguish, to make, to draw, to explain, to demonstrate	relevancies, relationships, essentials, aspects, new view(s), qualifications, conclusions, methods, theories, abstractions
2.30 Extrapolation	to estimate, to infer, to conclude, to predict, to differentiate, to determine, to extend, to interpolate, to extrapolate, to restructure	consequences, implications, conclusions, factors, ramifications, meanings, corollaries, effects, probabilities
3.00 Application	to apply, to generalize, to relate, to choose, to develop, to organize, to use, to employ, to transfer, to restructure, to classify	principles, laws, conclusions, effects, methods, theories, abstractions, situations, generalizations, processes, phenomena, procedures
4.00 Analysis		
4.10 Analysis of Elements	to distinguish, to detect, to identify, to classify, to discriminate, to recognize, to categorize, to deduce	elements, hypothesis/hypotheses, conclusions, assumptions, statements (of fact), statements (of intent), arguments, particulars

Taxonomy Classification	Key Words	
	Examples of Infinitives	Examples of Direct Objects
4.20 Analysis of Relationships	to analyze, to contrast, to compare, to distinguish, to deduce	relationships, inter-relationships, relevance, relevancies, themes, evidence, fallacies, arguments, cause-effect(s), consistency/consistencies, parts, ideas, assumptions
4.30 Analysis of Organizational Principles	to analyze, to distinguish, to detect, to deduce	form(s), pattern(s), purpose(s), point(s) of view(s), techniques, bias(es), structure(s), theme(s), arrangement(s), organization(s)
5.00 Synthesis		
5.10 Production of a Unique Communication	to write, to tell, to relate, to produce, to constitute, to transmit, to originate, to modify, to document	structure(s), pattern(s), product(s), perform-ance(s), design(s), work(s), communica-tion(s), effort(s), specifics, composition(s)
5.20 Production of a Plan, or Proposed Set of Operations	to propose, to plan, to produce, to design, to modify, to specify	plan(s), objectives, specifications(s), schematic(s), operations, ways, solution(s), means
5.30 Derivation of a Set of Abstract Relations	to produce, to derive, to develop, to combine, to organize, to synthesize, to classify, to deduce, to develop, to formulate, to modify	phenomena, taxonomies, concept(s), scheme(s), theories, relationships, abstractions, general-izations, hypothesis/hypotheses, perceptions, ways, discoveries
6.00 Evaluation		
6.10 Judgments in Terms of Internal Evidence	to judge, to argue, to validate, to assess, to decide	accuracy/accuracies, consistency/con-sistencies, fallacies, reliability, flaws, errors, precision, exactness
6.20 Judgments in Terms of External Criteria	to judge, to argue, to consider, to compare, to contrast, to standardize, to appraise	ends, means, efficiency, economy/economies, utility, alternatives, courses of action, standards, theories, generalizations

Tally Sheet				
Category	Segment			
	1	2	3	4
1.00 Knowledge of				
1.10 Specifics				
1.11 Terminology				
1.12 Specific facts				
1.20 Ways and means of dealing with specifics				
1.21 Conventions				
1.22 Trends, sequences				
1.23 Classifications and categories				
1.24 Criteria				
1.25 Methodology				
1.30 Universals and abstractions				
1.31 Principles and generalizations				
1.32 Theories and structure				
2.00 Comprehension				
2.10 Translation				
2.20 Interpretation				
2.30 Extrapolation				
3.00 Application				
4.00 Analysis of				
4.10 Elements				
4.20 Relationships				
4.30 Organizational principles				
5.00 Synthesis				
5.10 Production of a unique communication				
5.20 Production of a plan, or proposed set of operations				
5.30 Derivation of a set of abstract relations				
6.00 Evaluation				
6.10 Judgment in terms of internal evidence				
6.20 Judgment in terms of external criteria				

Relationship Between Students' Cognitive Functioning and the Teacher's Behavior

One of the central issues in education is the relationship between humaneness and academic achievement.[1,2,3] This is frequently expressed by the statement, "It's nice to be nice, but you've got to teach them something," reflecting a basic assumption that humaneness and the promotion of cognitive growth are antithetical. In an effort to examine this assumption, a study was made which investigated the relationship between teachers' classroom behavior and their students' levels of cognitive functioning.

The teachers' classroom behavior was subjected to interaction analysis using Flanders' categories.[4,5] The teachers' levels of interpersonal functioning were assessed by Carkhuff's Scales,[6] which were developed from the theoretical formulations of Carl Rogers;[7] i.e., that the facilitating effect of an interpersonal relationship is related directly and significantly to the levels of empathy, congruence, and positive regard provided by the helper. Although these assertions grew out of Rogers' experiences in psychotherapy, he extended them to include education. This position was supported by Aspy's[8] study in which the teacher's provision of the three facilitative conditions was found to be positively and significantly related to the students' cognitive gain as measured by Stanford Achievement Tests. In the present study, the students' levels of cognitive functioning were evaluated by an adaptation of a system reported by Metfessel, Michael, and Kirsner.[9] This procedure assesses the cognitive level of classrooms according to Bloom's Taxonomy of Educational Objectives[10] which differentiates the cognitive domain into six levels: (1) knowledge, (2) comprehension, (3) application, (4) analysis, (5) synthesis, and (6) evaluation.

Subjects

This study involved an assessment of the instruction of reading groups conducted by forty female elementary teachers. In the classroom groups of twenty of the teachers (Group I), the students remained at Level 1 of Bloom's Taxonomy throughout the hour, while the students of the other twenty teachers (Group II) attained one of the Levels 2 - 6. Thus, Group II may be characterized as teachers whose students achieved something other than memory and recall. The teachers who volunteered for this study were assured of anonymity, so it was not possible to match them for years of experience or educational level. The results are thus limited by the degree to which these variables were not randomly distributed. All of the classes were composed of students whose measured IQ's were between 90 and 120. The classrooms were located in schools whose students were predominantly from middle income families.

Procedure

Teaching samples. Each teacher tape recorded one hour of instruction with reading groups. The teachers had been directed to teach in their normal manner. These tape recordings were forwarded to our College of Education where they were evaluated blind by trained raters.

Assessment of teachers' interpersonal levels. The teachers' levels of interpersonal functioning were assessed blind by three trained raters who applied Carkhuff's Scales for Empathy, Congruence, and Positive Regard. Each of the raters completed their evaluations separately. The inter-rater reliabilities for all three scales were significant at .01, although the obtained Pearson's r's varied somewhat among the scales. (Empathy, $r = .83$; Congruence, $r = .76$; Positive Regard, $r = .79$.)

Four three-minute segments from each of the tapes were selected for evaluation by the raters. The first segment was taken from the beginning of the hour, the second segment from about twenty minutes into the hour, the third from about twenty minutes before the end of the hour, and the fourth segment at the end of the hour. The final rating used in the data analysis was the mean of the ratings by each of the raters for each of the four segments.

Assessment for interaction analysis. The same segments of each tape were used in the interaction analysis. All four three-minute segments from each of the tapes were coded by three trained raters using Flanders' Categories. Each of the raters completed their evaluations separately and inter-rater reliabilities were above .75 (p < .01). The data used in the analysis was the mean percent of time per category coded by each rater for all four segments.

Assessment of students' cognitive levels. The same segments used for the interaction analysis and the assessment of the teachers' levels of interpersonal functioning were also evaluated for the students' levels of cognitive functioning. The raters employed a procedure for obtaining levels of cognitive functioning adapted from Metfessel, Michael, and Kirsner's instrumentation of Bloom's Taxonomy. Each of the four three-minute segments per tape received a rating based on the highest levels of cognitive functioning achieved with significant frequency by the students during the segment. Inter-rater reliabilities were above .75. The ratings from this procedure were collapsed into two categories: (1) Level 1 of Bloom's Taxonomy and (2) Levels 2 - 6 of the taxonomy. Thus it was possible to investigate the differential interpersonal functioning of teachers whose students attained only Level 1 and those whose students attained Levels 2 - 6.

Results

The results are presented in Tables 1, 2, and 3. Table 1 indicates that the teacher's level of positive regard is the only interpersonal dimension which was judged significantly higher for the teachers whose students achieved cognitive levels 2 - 6. Displayed in Table 2 are the F-ratios obtained from nine ANOVA's performed in order to test the hypotheses of no significant difference in the levels of interpersonal

Table 1

Relationship Between Teacher Classroom Behavior Variables and Student Levels of Cognitive Functioning

Teacher Classroom Behavior Variables		Group I Cognitive Level 1 $\overline{X}_0$	Group II Cognitive Levels 2-6 $\overline{X}_1$	Total Teachers $\overline{X}.$	Biserial Coefficients	
					$s_X.$	r_{bis}
Flanders' Categories						
	1	0.00	0.05	0.025	0.1581	.2006
Indirect	2	2.10	1.80	1.950	2.76	-.0686
Influence	3	2.05	3.65	2.850	2.80	.3630*
	4	20.55	18.45	19.250	8.80	-.1155
	5	19.00	11.80	15.400	18.90	-.2418
Direct	6	10.15	8.65	9.400	8.98	-.1059
Influence	7	0.40	0.60	0.500	1.06	.1194
Student	8	31.20	28.00	29.600	16.87	-.1203
Talk	9	5.20	13.25	9.225	15.06	.3391*
Silence	10	9.25	12.65	10.950	11.52	.1872
Interpersonal Conditions						
Empathy		2.56	2.83	2.695	0.5315	.3223
Congruence		2.57	2.81	2.687	0.5679	.2626
Positive Regard		2.58	3.35	2.965	0.5950	.8213**

*Significant at .01   **Significant at .001

43

Table 2

Calculated *F*-ratios of Nine ANOVA's
Testing Equivalences Between Grade Level Means
of Teacher Interpersonal Functioning

Interpersonal Functioning Variables	Teachers Grouped by Cognitive Levels						Total Teachers		
	Level 1 Teachers			Level 2-6 Teachers					
	X	$\hat{\sigma}^2$	F*	X	$\hat{\sigma}^2$	F*	X	$\hat{\sigma}^2$	F**
Empathy	2.56	0.0152	1.45	2.83	0.0008	0.04	3.70	0.0033	0.45
Congruence	2.57	0.0241	1.66	2.80	0.0284	1.98	2.68	0.0125	1.57
Positive Regard	2.58	0.0088	1.46	3.37	0.0064	0.51	2.98	0.0029	0.33

$$* \quad F_{.95 \quad 3,16} = 3.24 \qquad ** \quad F_{.95 \quad 3,36} = 2.86$$

functioning by grade levels. Since none of the calculated *F*-values were significant, the data in Table 2 indicates that the levels of interpersonal functioning were not significantly related to the teacher's grade level. The biserial co-efficients by grade level in Table 3, taken in conjunction with the data in Table 2, indicate that the relationship between the teacher's level of interpersonal functioning and the students' level of cognitive functioning is not significantly related to grade level. On each grade level, the pattern is the same as that for the total group—only positive regard yields significant coefficients.

Summary and Discussion

This study investigated the relationship between the teacher's classroom behavior and the students' level of cognitive functioning. The data for the study was obtained from forty female elementary teachers who submitted an audio tape recording of one hour of their instruction of reading groups. Each teacher's performance was evaluated by three procedures: (1) Carkhuff's Scales for Empathy, Congruence, and Positive Regard; (2) Flanders' Interaction Analysis; and (3) level of cognitive functioning achieved by her students. The students of twenty teachers obtained only Level 1 of Bloom's Taxonomy of Educational Objectives, while the students of the other twenty teachers attained at least one of the other levels (2 - 6).

Table 3

Biserial Coefficients by Grade Level
for Relationships Between Teacher Interpersonal Functioning
and Student Level of Cognitive Functioning

Grade Levels	Interpersonal Functioning Variables		
	Empathy	Congruence	Positive Regard
3	-.1197	-.5836	.8952*
4	.4803	.5577	.9092*
5	.5768	.1429	1.0000*
6	.3459	.8027	.9312*

*Significant at .05.

An analysis of the relationship between the student levels of cognitive functioning and the teacher classroom behavior variables indicated that only the levels of Positive Regard provided by the teacher were significantly different for the two groups of teachers. The teachers whose students attained cognitive levels beyond Level 1 provided significantly higher levels of positive regard than those whose students remained at Level 1 throughout the hour.

In Aspy's previously cited study, all three interpersonal conditions (empathy, congruence, and positive regard) were found to be positively and significantly related to cognitive gain. As measured in that study (by standardized achievement tests), cognitive gain was an outcome of "product" variable the components of which were largely memory or recognition. In the present study, cognitive functioning was measured as a process variable and the focus was on the differential contributions of the various teacher behaviors to the attainment of levels of cognition beyond memory and recognition. Taken together, the two studies seem to indicate that all three interpersonal conditions facilitate cognitive gain, but that once the cognitive processes move beyond Level 1 (memory and recognition), positive regard is more directly facilitative of cognitive functioning or "thinking" as a process within the instructional situation.

While not definitive, this study seems important for two reasons. First, it indicates that a teacher's increased positive regard for students is translated into classroom behavior which elicits higher levels of cognitive functioning from the students. That is, the teacher successfully facilitates student use of cognitive behavior which we commonly call "thinking."

Perhaps one ingredient of a classroom environment conducive to productive cognitive functioning is the "right to be wrong," i.e., the recognition by the student that the teacher regards him as a worthwhile individual with a unique contribution to make to the class and that his participation will be respected even though it may not be "correct" in terms of the lesson at hand. Such an environment would seem to lower the "risk" to the student involved in going beyond memory and recognition to the "less certain" levels of critical and creative thinking. Although not at an acceptable level of significance ($p < .10$), the correlation (see Table 1) between high levels of cognitive functioning and Flanders' Category 3 (Accepts or Uses Ideas of Students) would seem to support the above interpreation of the meaning of positive regard within the instructional group, while the correlation with Category 9 (Student Initiated Talk) seems to indicate that there may well be some relationship between willingness to "risk" and "thinking" behavior.

A second significant aspect of this study is that it demonstrates a procedure which can be applied to many situations for investigating the important issue of the relationship between the teacher's interpersonal facilitation and student levels of cognitive functioning. It may well turn out that "It's nice to be nice, and it also teaches something."

1. Aspy, D. N. Maslow and teachers in training. *The Journal of Teacher Education,* 1969, *20* (3), 362-369.

2. Association for Supervision and Curriculum Development, NEA. *Life Skills in School and Society,* prepared by the ASCD Yearbook Committee. Louis J. Rubin, chairman and editor. Washington, D. C.: National Education Association, 1969.

3. Rogers, C. R. *Freedom to learn.* Columbus, Ohio: Charles E. Merrill Co., 1969.

4. Amidon, E. J. and Flanders, N. A. *The role of the teacher in the classroom: A manual for understanding and improving teachers' classroom behavior.* Minneapolis, Minnesota: Amidon and Associates, 1963.

5. Flanders, N. A. *Teacher influence, pupil attitudes and achievement.* U. S. Department of Health, Education and Welfare, Cooperative Research Monograph No. 12. Washington, D. C.: Government Printing Office, 1965.

6. Carkhuff, R. R. *Helping and human relations: A primer for lay and professional helpers. Vol. I. Selection and training. Vol. II. Practice and research.* New York: Holt, Rinehart and Winston, 1969.

7. Rogers, C. R. *On becoming a person.* Boston: Houghton Mifflin, 1961.

8. Aspy, D. N. The effect of teacher-offered conditions of empathy, positive regard, and congruence upon student achievement. *Florida Journal of Educational Research,* 1969, *11* (1), 39-48. Also abstracted in *Beyond counseling and therapy* (R. R. Carkhuff and B. C. Berenson) New York: Holt, Rinehart and Winston, 1967.

9. Metfessel, N. S., Michael, W.B., Kirsner, D.A. Instrumentation of Bloom's and Krathwohl's taxonomies for the writing of educational objectives. *Psychology in the Schools,* 1969, *7* (3), 227-231.

10. Bloom, B. S. (Ed.), Englehart, M. D., Furst, E. J., Hill, W. H., and Krathwohl, D. R., *A taxonomy of educational objectives: Handbook I, The cognitive domain.* New York: Longmans, Green, 1956.

Empathy: 4
IN HUMANE CLASSROOMS
STUDENTS' FEELINGS COUNT

Empathy, the sensing of another person's inner world of private personal meanings, has been discussed mainly as the measure of one person's ability to predict another's performance in a particular situation. Patterson expresses this view in the following:

> Most attempts to measure empathy have been along the lines of determining the extent to which the subject has entered the internal frame of reference of another by appraising his success in predicting aspects of the other's behavior, feelings, or attitudes.[1]

Since most of the work related to empathy has involved prediction, most of the literature reported will pertain to empathy in this frame of reference, but the definition adopted for this study places empathy in a communication frame of reference in that it is measured as a part of a moment-by-moment process. It may be that these two quantities are similar, but it seems that prediction involves a greater degree of the cognitive domain than the affective domain while the reverse is true for spontaneous communication.

Joslin found a difference between cognitive knowledge and counselors' competence:

> The low correlation between knowledge and counseling competence provides evidence for doubting the effectiveness of counselor education programs that are composed entirely of didactic courses. From the present findings there is little reason to believe that students become highly competent counselors.[2]

Combs and Soper investigated "good" and "bad" teachers' concepts of the ideal helping relationship and drew this conclusion:

> It is not enough to help students see more clearly what good helping relationships are like. Apparently, they know already!... There is a great difference between "knowing" and

"behaving" and the successful teachers' college cannot be content with producing mere changes in "knowing" ... apparently, helping relationships are not markedly different wherever they are found. This means that training programs for counselors, psychotherapists, social workers, nurses, and all other helping professions, including teaching, are engaged in the same basic process.[3]

The *National Education Association Journal*'s discussion of the classroom climate affirms the importance of moment-by-moment interaction:

No matter how much a teacher may have read and studied he still has to discover for himself the ways in which children perceive facts and ideas at different ages. In addition, the familiar experience in a child's home and community life may be quite different from what the teacher has known. The application of this knowledge requires constant split-second decisions in the midst of busy classroom life.[4]

Buchheimer seems both pessimistic and optimistic about the usefulness of investigative empathy:

Empathic processes have been studied from only a limited point of view and as a consequence we still do not have a dependable test for empathy. Empathy is talked about more today than it was ten years ago, but to date there is no measure of empathy that has either social, industrial, educational, or therapeutic usefulness.[5]

He supports the differentiation between predictive and interactional empathy:

A study among 21 counselor trainees found a negative Rho of -.39 between predictive and interactive empathy (t = 1.89 approaching the .05 level of confidence). Katz's results confirm Cartwright's and this writer's contention that empathic prediction and empathic interaction should be studied separately.[6]

He proposes further investigation of empathy:

For the study of empathic interaction, situational tests such as those devised by Astin, Arbuckle, and Wicas, or Weinstein and McCandless, may be fruitful techniques for studying empathic responsiveness.[7]

Dixon and Morse's definition of empathy indicates its dynamic characteristic:

The important aspect of empathy, as we recognize it in teaching, is a highly interpersonal phenomenon with the subject and object bound up in a mutual response.[8]

Olden indicates this same dynamic, spontaneous quality:

> Empathy is the capacity of the subject instinctively and intuitively to feel as the object does. . .empathy may be described as a feeling that emerges spontaneously in social contact, that enables the subject instantaneously to sense the object's apparent emotions. . .to trespass the object's screen of defenses behind which the real feelings may hide.[9]

Lewis and Wigel discuss the "intensely human" quality of empathy:

> The evidence . . . suggests that those who are perceived as being understanding have no better intellectual understanding of a subject than those who are perceived as not being understanding . . . if we intend to stimulate in others a feeling of being understood, it is not important that we gain considerable information about them but rather that we help them see that we are able to perceive others and situations as they do.[10]

Dixon and Morse administered tests to 97 student teachers in an attempt to assess their empathic potential and later asked their students (2000) to assess the student teachers' understanding of them. They found the following:

1. "Good" empathy teachers were rated as better teachers by the pupils than were the poor empathy teachers.
2. Supervising teachers see the good empathy groups as being significantly better teachers than the "poor" groups.
3. There was no significant difference between the overall self-ratings of the "good" and "poor" group.
4. Student teachers who developed very positive feelings toward their pupils were significantly more stable in their appraisal of themselves as teachers.[11]

Gage reports in the *Handbook of Research on Teaching* that Thelen's monographs:

> . . . emphasized the need to examine the understanding of the individual learner's frame of reference within the context of the group values and pressures in the classroom situation. This understanding requires the development by the teacher of ability to hypothesize the internal frame of reference of each learner (a kind of "empathy" as interpersonal perception) and to ascertain how she can use group forces and group problem-solving mechanisms to bring about learning.[12]

Gage proposes cautious evaluation of the significance of understanding of pupils:

> Our negative results should cause us to look more closely at what

we mean by understanding of pupils. Such understanding is a basic objective of teacher education curricula. . . . It is indeed highly plausible as a desideratum for teachers. Yet up to now, in our own . . . and in others' research, support for this proposition has been hard to come by.[13]

Gage and Suci found a positive relationship (r = .50) between the teachers' accurate social perception and the pupils' mean favorability toward the teacher.[14]

Stephens reports that:

The evidence on this topic, although somewhat conflicting, does not suggest that a more intimate knowledge of pupils typically leads to superior teaching.[15]

He cites that Hoyt found that increased understanding of pupils did not lead to gains in achievement, although it did lead to occasional improvement in the pupils' attitudes toward the teacher. However, he concludes by saying:

Along with the studies directly attacking this problem there is some evidence which must suggest the wisdom of keeping an open mind on this question (understanding and learning).[16]

There seems to be a consensus among the writers cited that: (1) there is a need for a measure of empathy as an ongoing, dynamic process; (2) cognitive understanding appears to differ from interactional empathy; (3) the classroom effect of "understanding the pupil" seems to be related to students' evaluation of teachers; (4) there is a need for further investigation of the construct of empathy within the classroom context.

Empathy in a Classroom Interaction

The following example is presented to illustrate the role of empathic understanding in the classroom interaction:

Student: Why've we gotta do this stuff?
Teacher: You don't like this assignment, do you?
Student: No. It seems irrelevant.
Teacher: You can't see much meaning for you in this.
Student: Yeah. I don't like to give oral reports. How come I can't do a written one?
Teacher: You're more comfortable writing than you are speaking to a group.
Student: I. . .I'm not much good at talking.

Teacher:	You'd rather do what you can do well than try something where you feel uncomfortable.
Student:	Sure! 'Sides, people always laugh when I give an oral report.
Teacher:	You've had a lot of bad experiences speaking and you feel sure it'll be the same in this class.
Student:	It's always been that way. I don't see why this will be any different.
Teacher:	You're judging this class by others you've attended. . . .You feel that I'll let the same thing happen to you.
Student:	Yeah. Most teachers seem pretty much alike.
Teacher:	You think that since I'm a teacher I'm going to try to hurt you.
Student:	I've never been the teacher's pet . . . . We don't get along very well.
Teacher:	You've never met a teacher who likes you . . . one you could trust, and you don't expect me to like you or trust you.
Student:	I don't see why you should . . . . I'm a lousy student.
Teacher:	You don't think I could like a student who has always made poor grades.
Student:	Most teachers don't like you if you make bad grades.
Teacher:	That's not the way it ought to be though, is it? You feel very deeply that you've been mistreated by lots of teachers.
Student:	Yeah. I'm as good as those smart people . . . .
Teacher:	This has hurt a lot, I'm sure.
Student:	There are lots of times when I'd like to quit, but you can't get a good job without an education.
Teacher:	You feel kinda trapped between school and life outside school.
Student:	I wish there was some way I could like school . . . . I really would like to learn something.
Teacher:	Maybe we can start in this class. I'd like to help you learn what is important to you. Suppose you think about what you'd like to do and we'll talk about it tomorrow, O.K.?
Student:	O.K. Hope I didn't make you mad.
Teacher:	You know, I hope we'll always be able to be honest with each other. That's what's important to me. I feel like we really met each other today, and I think we can work together. I'd like to try.
Student:	See ya tomorrow.

The real problem emerged only as the teacher tried to understand the deeper feelings of the student. An alternative approach could have proceeded as follows:

Student: Why do we have to do this stuff?

Teacher: I know you don't understand the need for this kind of work, but it'll be clearer as the term moves along. You know, when you get to high school you'll need this sort of experience.

This second approach not only demeans the student, but also leaves the basic problem untouched. You see, this kind of understanding is necessary if learning is to proceed with maximum efficiency.

Measuring a Teacher's Understanding of Students' Experiences

Using the In-Service Training Scale

The in-service training scale to follow measures a teacher's understanding of the meaning of classroom experiences for her students. The primary purpose of this scale is to indicate to teachers that each student has a personal world in which he experiences not only substantive material but also his feelings about the content. In other words, the student is emotional as well as academic, and when we respond to his personal meanings, it increases his total learning. Therefore, the focus of the in-service training program is the enhancement of the teacher's abilities to both understand and respond to the meaning of the student's experience to himself.

The training sessions usually consist of the following steps:

1. A trainer makes a didactic explanation of empathy (understanding) and the scale.
2. The group listens to standard audio tape recordings of different teachers and rates them according to the scale. The ratings are discussed and the trainer continues this procedure until the group seems proficient in the use of the scale.
3. The group, if large, is divided into small groups (4 or 5) and volunteers audio tape record their teaching and bring the tape to the meeting to be rated by the entire group. This procedure is repeated as long as it seems productive for the group.

Since the central focus of the in-service training scale is communication rather than precision, the training sessions are not primarily concerned with statistical reliability, so the trainer concentrates on the trainees' apparent understanding of the dimension and the scale.

In-Service Training Scale: Teacher's Understanding of Students' Classroom Experiences.

Level 1
Neither the tonal quality nor the words of the teacher's verbal communication conveys any feelings, and/or she responds inaccurately to the meaning of the students' experiences.

Examples: (1) The tone of the teacher's voice is flat or monotonous.

             (2) The teacher says, "You enjoyed that" after a student's performance indicates obvious dislike for the activity.

Level 2
The tone of the teacher's verbal communication conveys slight evidence of feelings which are only somewhat appropriate to her students' experience. She uses no words to explicate her feelings.

Examples: (1) The teacher's voice is very subdued and controlled.

             (2) The teacher says, "Let's hold it down" after a student expresses joy with the activity.

Level 3
The tonal quality of the teacher's verbal communication conveys feelings which are quite appropriate to her students' experiences. She is "with" her students. However, she uses no words to explicate her feelings.

Examples: (1) The teacher's voice matches that of her students. She neither adds nor detracts from the meaning of their experience.

             (2) The teacher says "Good" after a student demonstrates appropriate joy with the activity.

Level 4
The tone of the teacher's verbal communication conveys feelings which are appropriate to her students' experiences. Additionally, she uses mild words to describe the feelings.

Examples: (1) The teacher adds slightly to the meaning of the students' experience by appropriate words.

             (2) The teacher says, "Good, you seemed to really enjoy that!" after a student demonstrates appropriate joy with the activity.

Level 5
The tone of the teacher's verbal communication conveys feelings which are appropriate to her students' experiences. Additionally, she uses "strong" words to describe her feelings.

Examples: (1) The teacher adds a great deal to the meaning of the students' experience by appropriate words.

(2) The teacher says, "Great, I felt like you were going to dance you liked that so much!" after a student demonstrates appropriate joy with the activity.

Using the Carkhuff Scale for Empathic Understanding

The Carkhuff Scale is more detailed and precise than the in-service training scale, and, therefore, requires more preparation. Training, of course, is the most effective vehicle for learning both the discrimination and communication of interpersonal dimensions.[17] However, since teachers often have a limited amount of time for training, it has been found that the Carkhuff Scale may be employed meaningfully in the following sequence:

1. Teachers learn to use the in-service training scale for student meaning.
2. A trainer makes a didactic explanation of the Carkhuff Scale for Empathic Understanding.
3. The teachers audio tape record their teaching and send the tape to be evaluated by experienced raters.
4. The teachers receive reports of the assessments by the raters.

A local school system may also want to provide a rating service for its schools and teachers, and, if so, it is recommended that they either employ someone who has been trained to use the scales previously or secure a trainer to prepare at least three local personnel to do so.

Precision is a concern of the Carkhuff Scale and inter-rater and intra-rater reliabilities are important. Since the usual rating procedure involves three raters working independently, it is important that they are trained effectively and, also, that they stay in communication with each other as they continue to rate. This latter step insures an on-going in-service program for the raters.

Carkhuff Scale: Empathic Understanding in Interpersonal Processes*

Level 1
The verbal and behavioral expressions of the first person either *do not attend to* or *detract significantly from* the verbal and behavioral

---

*The present scale "Empathic Understanding in Interpersonal Processes" has been derived in part from "A Scale for the Measurement of Accurate Empathy" by C. B. Truax which has been validated in extensive process and outcome research

56

expressions of the second person(s) in that they communicate significantly less of the second person's feelings than the second person has communicated himself.

Example: The first person communicates no awareness of even the most obvious, expressed surface feelings of the second person. The first person may be bored or disinterested or simply operating from a preconceived frame of reference which totally excludes that of the other person(s).

In summary, the first person does everything but express that he is listening, understanding, or being sensitive to even the feelings of the other person in such a way as to detract significantly from the communications of the second person.

Level 2

While the first person responds to the expressed feelings of the second person(s), he does so in such a way that he *subtracts noticeable affect* from the communications of the second person.

Example: The first person may communicate some awareness of obvious surface feelings of the second person but his communications drain off a level of the affect and distort the level of meaning. The first person may communicate his own ideas of what may be going on but these are not congruent with the expressions of the second person.

In summary, the first person tends to respond to other than what the second person is experiencing and expressing.

Level 3

The expressions of the first person in response to the expressed feelings of the second person(s) are essentially interchangeable with those of the second person in that they express essentially the same affect and meaning.

---

on counseling and psychotherapy (summarized in Truax and Carkhuff[18]) and in part from an earlier version which has been validated in extensive process and outcome research on counseling and psychotherapy (summarized in Carkhuff and Berenson[19]). In addition, similar measures of similar constructs have received extensive support in the literature of counseling and therapy and education. The present scale was written to apply to all interpersonal processes and represent a systematic attempt to reduce the ambiguity and increase the reliability of the scale. In the process many important delineations and additions have been made, including in particular the change to a systematic focus upon the additive, subtractive, or interchangeable aspects of the levels of communication of understanding. For comparative purposes, Level 1 of the present scale is approximately equal to Stage 1 of the Truax Scale. The remaining levels are approximately correspondent: Level 2 and Stages 2 and 3 of the earlier version; Level 3 and Stages 4 and 5; Level 4 and Stages 6 and 7; Level 5 and Stages 8 and 9. The levels of the present scale are approximately equal to the levels of the earlier version of this scale.

Example: The first person responds with accurate understanding of the surface feelings of the second person but may not respond to or may misinterpret the deeper feelings.

In summary, the first person is responding so as to neither subtract from nor add to the expressions of the second person; but he does not respond accurately to how that person really feels beneath the surface feelings. Level 3 constitutes the minimal level of facilitative interpersonal functioning.

Level 4

The responses of the first person *add noticeably* to the expressions of the second person(s) in such a way as to express feelings a level deeper than the second person was able to express himself.

Example: The facilitator communicates his understanding of the expressions of the second person at a level deeper than they were expressed, and thus enables the second person to experience and/or express feelings which he was unable to express previously.

In summary, the facilitator's responses add deeper feeling and meaning to the expressions of the second person.

Level 5

The first person's responses add significantly to the feeling and meaning of the expressions of the second person(s) in such a way as to (1) accurately express feelings levels below what the person himself was able to express or (2) in the event of ongoing deep self-exploration on the second person's part, to be fully with him in his deepest moments.

Example: The facilitator responds with accuracy to all of the person's deeper as well as surface feelings. He is "together" with the second person or "tuned in" on his wave length. The facilitator and the other person might proceed together to explore previously unexplored areas of human existence.

In summary, the facilitator is responding with a full awareness of who the other person is and a comprehensive and accurate empathic understanding of his deepest feelings.

The Effect of Teacher-Offered Empathy
Upon Student Achievement

There is extensive evidence to suggest that all interpersonal learning or relearning processes share the same core of conditions offered by the "more knowing" person to the "less knowing" person. In particular, the condition of empathy has been related to constructive client change or gain in guidance, counseling, and therapy by Aspy,[20] Carkhuff,[21,22] Rogers,[23] and Truax and Carkhuff.[24] Indirect evidence has been presented for the effect of this condition in teaching by Bowers and Soar,[25] Christenson,[26] Combs and Soper,[27] Cronbach,[28] Garrison, Kingston, and McDonald,[29] Ryans,[30] Tatum,[31] Thelen,[32] Melton,[33] Morgan,[34] and Willis.[35] Unfortunately, none of the studies of the effectiveness of teaching have systematically explored the relationship of the condition of empathy to teaching effectiveness. It is the purpose of this study, then, to (a) assess the levels of empathy that teachers are communicating, and (b) determine the differential effects of this condition upon the cognitive growth of students as assessed by achievement tests.

Methodology

Teachers. Six third grade teachers tape recorded their interaction with reading groups during one week in March and one week in May of the same academic year. The recordings were done as randomly as possible to account for such influences as time of day and day of week.

Subjects. The subjects were selected from the teachers' classes and included (a) the five boys with the highest IQ's, (b) the five boys with the lowest IQ's, (c) the five girls with the highest IQ's and (d) the five girls with the lowest IQ's. Thus, twenty students were selected from each teacher's class. The differences between the mean IQ's for each of the low groups were non-significant, and the same was true for the high groups. That is, all the high IQ groups and all the low IQ groups were statistically equated since their differences were non-significant. Of course, there were significant differences between the high and low groups. The selection process controlled for sex and IQ.

The students were administered five subtests of the Stanford Achievement Test during September and again during May of the same academic year. The differences between the subjects' scores were used as the measure of the students' academic gain. The subtests were (a) Word Meaning, (b) Paragraph Meaning, (c) Spelling, (d) Word Study Skills, and (e) Language, all of which relate to verbal quantities. This seemed appropriate since the teachers were recording their reading groups which are verbal situations.

Ratings. The teachers had recorded two hours of classroom interaction, and eight four-minute segments were selected randomly from each teacher's performance. These segments were assigned numbers randomly, so the raters identified them only by their numbers.

Three trained raters, experienced at evaluating recordings of counseling and psychotherapy, assessed the levels of empathy provided by the teachers on each of the segments. The ratings for each teacher were summed and a composite or mean rating for each teacher was obtained.

The rating scales were designed to allow trained but otherwise naive raters to evaluate the levels of empathy provided by a therapist.[36] The raters formulated their opinions by listening to randomly selected samples from psychotherapeutic interviews.

Accurate Empathy (AE) is assessed according to a 9-point scale with a rating of 1 representing the lowest level of empathy and 9 the highest. At Stage 1 the therapist seems completely unaware of even the most conspicuous of the client's feelings. His responses are not appropriate to the mood and content of the client's statement and there is no determinable quality of empathy. At Stage 3, the therapist often responds accurately to the client's more exposed feelings. He also displays concern for the deeper, more hidden feelings, which he seems to sense must be present though he doesn't understand their nature. At Stage 5, the therapist accurately responds to all of the client's more readily discernible feelings. He shows awareness of many of the feelings and experiences which are not so evident, too; but in these he tends to be somewhat inaccurate in his understanding. At Stage 7, the therapist shows awareness of the precise intensity of the underlying emotions. However, his responses move only slightly beyond the area of the client's own awareness, so that feelings may be present which are not recognized by the client or therapist. At Stage 9, the therapist unerringly responds to the client's full range of feelings in their exact intensity. He expands the client's hint into a full-blown but tentative elaboration of feeling or experience with unerring sensitivity and accuracy.

Results

The mean rating for each of the six teachers on the dimension of accurate empathy is summarized in Table 1.

Since teachers 1, 2, and 3 received higher ratings than teachers 4, 5, and 6, the following categories were used in the analysis of the data:

60

high condition teachers (1, 2, and 3), and low condition teachers (4, 5, and 6). The term facilitative condition was implemented in the discussion of the analysis of the data.

Table 1

Mean Rating for Accurate Empathy

Teacher	Accurate Empathy
1	4.7
2	3.9
3	3.5
4	3.0
5	2.9
6	2.3

The achievement test results are summarized in Tables 2 through 7.

Table 2

Mean Gain Score for Paragraph Meaning for Each Group

Teacher	Male High IQ	Low IQ	Female High IQ	Low IQ	Average by Teachers	Level of Conditions
1	1.68	.66	.76	.40	.88	High
2	1.22	.32	1.44	1.32	1.08	High
3	1.12	.44	1.44	1.00	1.00	High
4	1.10	.74	.80	.68	.83	Low
5	.58	.22	.40	.28	.37	Low
6	1.02	.74	.76	.64	.79	Low
Average for IQ Groups	1.12	.52	.93	.72	Average for Entire Group	0.82

Note: The test norms indicate that the gain by the average third grade student is 1.0 years.

Table 3

Mean Gain Score for Language for Each Group

Teacher	Male High IQ	Male Low IQ	Female High IQ	Female Low IQ	Average by Teachers	Level of Condition
1	2.04	.78	1.16	.44	1.11	High
2	2.30	.90	2.88	1.78	1.97	High
3	1.70	1.24	1.26	1.12	1.33	High
4	.70	.58	1.18	.92	.85	Low
5	1.04	.42	.84	.18	.62	Low
6	.00	.40	1.36	.74	.62	Low
Average for IQ Groups	1.30	.72	1.45	.86	Average for Entire Group	1.08

Note: The test norms indicate that the gain by the average third grade student is 1.0 years.

Table 4

Mean Gain Score for Word Meaning for Each Group

Teacher	Male High IQ	Male Low IQ	Female High IQ	Female Low IQ	Average by Teachers	Level of Condition
1	1.44	.98	.76	.82	1.00	High
2	1.44	.82	.86	1.32	1.11	High
3	1.30	.56	.66	.60	.79	High
4	1.28	.30	.90	.70	.80	Low
5	1.28	.20	.76	.72	.74	Low
6	.62	.70	1.06	.60	.75	Low
Average for IQ Groups	1.23	.60	.83	.79	Average for Entire Group	.86

Note: The test norms indicate that the gain by the average third grade student is 1.0 years.

Table 5

Mean Gain Score for Word Study Skills for Each Group

Teacher	Male		Female		Average by Teachers	Levels of Conditions
	High IQ	Low IQ	High IQ	Low IQ		
1	1.78	1.74	1.94	.74	1.55	High
2	2.00	.08	2.24	2.44	1.69	High
3	.16	.82	.98	.18	.46	High
4	.88	1.02	.78	.76	.86	Low
5	1.36	.80	.44	.12	.62	Low
6	1.50	.08	.72	.96	.82	Low
Average for IQ Groups	1.23	.76	1.18	.83	Average for Entire Group	1.00

Note: The test norms indicate that the gain by the average third grade student is 1.0 years.

Table 6

Mean Gain Score for Spelling for Each Group

Teacher	Male		Female		Average by Teachers	Levels of Conditions
	High IQ	Low IQ	High IQ	Low IQ		
1	1.00	.92	1.08	.50	.87	High
2	1.42	.18	1.22	1.68	1.12	High
3	.52	1.30	.78	.74	.83	High
4	.94	1.14	1.80	1.26	1.28	Low
5	1.38	.66	1.24	.58	.96	Low
6	.92	.88	1.22	1.22	1.06	Low
Average for IQ Groups	1.03	.84	1.22	.99	Average for Entire Group	1.02

Note: The test norms indicate that the gain by the average third grade student is 1.0 years.

Table 7

Mean Gain Score for Total for Each Group

| Teacher | Male | | Female | | Average by | Levels of |
	High IQ	Low IQ	High IQ	Low IQ	Teachers	Condition
1	8.54	5.22	5.76	2.96	5.62	High
2	8.38	2.50	8.64	8.54	7.01	High
3	4.48	4.34	5.20	3.50	4.38	High
4	4.50	3.78	5.46	4.32	4.51	Low
5	5.94	2.74	3.68	1.68	3.51	Low
6	3.96	2.88	5.12	4.16	4.03	Low
Average for IQ Groups	5.96	2.57	5.64	4.19	Average for Entire Group	4.84

Note: The test norms indicate that the total gain for five subtests by the average third grade student is 5.0 years.

As can be observed, in Paragraph Meaning, Language, Word Meaning, and Word Study Skills the average amount gained by the students of the high level functioning teachers was substantially more than that of students of those teachers offering low level of the condition, while on Spelling the differences are negative but minimal. Overall, on the total gain, the students of the high level teachers demonstrated greater gain than those of low level teachers. An analysis of variance for each of the subjects yielded the results summarized in Table 8.

Summary and Conclusions

The levels of empathy provided by teachers in their actual classroom procedure related positively to the cognitive growth of their students. This positive relationship was found for four subtests of the Stanford Achievement Test and the total gain. These relationships were statistically significant at or above the .05 level of confidence. For the Spelling subtest the teacher condition was related negatively to the test score gains, but the relationship was not statistically significant at the .05 level of confidence.

This study supports the general hypothesis that there is a positive relationship between the levels of teacher-offered empathy and the cognitive growth of the students. It extends the generalization of the

Table 8

A Summary of the Statistical Significance of the Sources of Variance

Source	Total Gain	Paragraph Meaning	Language	Word Meaning	Word Study Skills	Spelling
1. IQ	.01	.01	.01	.01	.01	N.S.
2. Level of facilitating condition	.01	.01	.001	.05	.01	N.S.
3. Sex	N.S.	N.S.	N.S.	N.S.	N.S.	N.S.
4. IQ and facilitating condition	N.S.	N.S.	N.S.	N.S.	N.S.	N.S.
5. IQ and sex	N.S.	N.S.	N.S.	.01	N.S.	N.S.
6. Facilitating condition and sex	N.S.	N.S.	N.S.	N.S.	N.S.	N.S.
7. IQ, facilitating condition, and sex	N.S.	N.S.	N.S.	N.S.	N.S.	N.S.
8. Teachers within level of facilitating condition	.01	N.S.	N.S.	N.S.	.01	N.S.
9. Teachers and sex within levels of facilitating condition	.01	N.S.	N.S.	N.S.	N.S.	N.S.
10. Teachers and IQ within levels of facilitating condition	N.S.	N.S.	N.S.	N.S.	N.S.	N.S.
11. Teachers, sex, and IQ within levels of facilitating condition	N.S.	N.S.	N.S.	N.S.	N.S.	N.S.

N.S. = Non Significant

effect of empathy to all instances of interpersonal learning processes. In particular, it points up the need for assessing teachers on other than intellective indices. However, while assessments were made independent of teacher knowledge ability, it is also quite possible that those offering the highest levels of empathy were most knowledgeable, and future studies should incorporate such necessary controls. In addition there are further questions which must be asked. Is, for example, the level of empathy offered by the teacher more critical during the early grammar school years than in later phases of education? In any event, this project can serve as a model for further research into the effectiveness of teaching, and if replicated, the results of this study have potentially profound implications for teaching and teacher-training programs.

1. Patterson, C. H. Note on the construct validity of the concept of empathy. *Personnel and Guidance Journal,* 1962, *40,* 803-806.

2. Joslin, L. C. Knowledge and counseling competence. *Personnel and Guidance Journal,* 1965, *43* (8), 790-795.

3. Combs, A. W. and Soper, D. L. Helping relationships as described by good and bad teachers. *Journal of Teacher Education,* 1963, *14,* 64-67.

4. Building a classroom climate for learning. *NEA Journal,* December, 1961, *50,* 34-8.

5. Buchheimer, A. Development of ideas about empathy. *Journal of Counseling Psychology,* 1963, *10,* 61-70.

6. *Ibid.*

7. *Ibid.*

8. Dixon, W. R. and Morse, W. C. Prediction of teaching performance: Empathic potential. *Journal of Teacher Education,* 1961, *12,* 322-329.

9. Olden, C. Adult empathy with children. *Psychoanalytic Study of the Child,* New York: International University Press, 1953, *8,* 115.

10. Lewis, W. A. and Wigel, W. Interpersonal understanding and assumed similarity. *Personnel and Guidance Journal,* 1964, *43* (2), 155-158.

11. Dixon and Morse, *op cit.*

12. Gage, N. L. *Handbook of research on teaching.* Chicago: Rand-McNally, 1963.

13. *Ibid.*

14. *Ibid.*

15. Stephens, J. M. *The psychology of classroom learning.* New York: Holt, Rinehart and Winston, 1965.

16. *Ibid.*

17. Carkhuff, R. R. *Helping and human relations: A primer for lay and professional helpers. Vol. I. Selection and training. Vol. II. Practice and research.* New York: Holt, Rinehart and Winston, 1969.

18. Truax, C. B. and Carkhuff, R. R. *Toward effective counseling and psychotherapy.* Chicago: Aldine, 1967.

19. Carkhuff, R. R. and Berenson, B. *Beyond counseling and therapy.* New York: Holt, Rinehart and Winston, 1968.

20. Aspy, D. N. Counseling and education. In R. Carkhuff (Ed.), *The counselor's contribution to facilitative processes.* Urbana, Illinois: R. W. Parkinson-Follett, 1967.

21. Carkhuff, R. R. Training in the counseling and therapeutic processes: Requiem or reveille? *Journal of Counseling Psychology,* 1966, *13,* 360-367.

22. Carkhuff, R. R. Toward explaining success or failure in interpersonal learning experiences. *Personnel and Guidance Journal,* 1966, *44,* 723-728.

23. Rogers, C. R. The interpersonal relationship: The core of guidance. *Harvard Educational Review,* 1962, *32,* 416-429.

24. Truax and Carkhuff, *op. cit.*

25. Bowers, N. E. and Soar, R. S. Influence of teacher personality on classroom interaction. *Journal of Experimental Education,* 1962, *30,* 309-311.

26. Christenson, C. M. Relationships between pupil achievement, pupil affect-need, teacher warmth and teacher permissiveness, *Journal of Educational Psychology,* 1960, *51,* 169-174.

27. Combs and Soper, *op. cit.*

28. Cronbach, L. J. *Educational psychology.* New York: Harcourt, Brace and World, 1963.

29. Garrison, K. C., Kingston, A. J., and McDonald, A. S. *Educational psychology.* New York: Appleton-Century-Crofts, 1964.

30. Ryans, D. R. Inventory estimated teacher characteristics as covariants of observer assessed pupil behavior. *Journal of Educational Psychology,* 1961, *52,* 91-97.

31. Tatum, C. D. Study completed at the University of Kentucky, 1965.

32. Thelen, A. H. One small head. *Journal of Teacher Education,* 1961, *12,* 401-406.

33. Melton, C. The helping relationship in college reading clinics. *Personnel and Guidance Journal,* 1955, *18,* 925-928.

34. Morgan, H. G. How to facilitate learning. *NEA Journal,* 1960, *49,* 54-55.

35. Willis, N. *The guinea pigs after 20 years.* Columbus, Ohio: Ohio State University, 1961.

36. Truax and Carkhuff, *op. cit.*

Congruence: 5
IN HUMANE CLASSROOMS
TEACHERS ARE AUTHENTIC

The literature related to congruence or genuineness in classrooms is scarce indeed. This is regrettable and challenging since ingenuineness creates ambiguity which in turn creates anxiety.

The *National Education Association Journal* stated:

> In dealing with children there is no room for pretense. The teacher must be honest with himself as well as his children. He must use his authority wisely, grant approval only when it is deserved and then in such a way that it furthers the child's next efforts toward learning.[1]

Stephens refers to sincerity when he says:

> We have suggested that the praise should be reasonably appropriate. This will probably vary with the students being taught. Young children can unembarrassedly accept praise for quite an ordinary performance . . . here the most useful test would probably be that of sincerity. If you do feel an admiration for the students' performance, give free vent to your feelings.[2]

Bowers and Soar by studying teachers' performance on the Minnesota Multiphasic Personality Inventory and the classroom procedure concluded this:

> A teacher must care, must not have this concern blocked by her own intrapersonal tensions, and must be relatively free of distorting mechanisms and able to enter honestly into relationships with others. Perhaps what this reduces to is that a teacher must be able to use her "self" openly, clearly, and honestly in her interactions with pupils.[3]

Thurman seems to express the behavioral manifestations of "being yourself." "When this happens (acceptance) you are free to be yourself without pretending to be someone else—you do not have to stretch yourself out of shape. You can be you, whole and complete."[4]

Stansfield's statement about teacher honesty seems to refer to a kind of intellectual congruence:

> As teachers we have an obligation to be intellectually honest with our students at all times while at the same time remaining calm and friendly.[5]

This appears to separate intellectual honesty from emotional honesty since the teacher's honest or congruent response might be quite angry and upset.

Bills supports the thesis that genuineness is important:

> If a teacher communicates to a child attitudes such as, "I dislike you," "I think you are not very worthwhile," "I don't think you are important enough to try to understand," and so forth, the relationship will not be one in which a child can become more intelligent. Even more harmful is the teacher who holds these beliefs and attempts to act as if he didn't. People are always more upset by conflicting messages from other people than by predictable messages even though these may invariably be negative.[6]

He states clearly that genuine people, even those who hold negative views of us, are more constructive (perhaps not as destructive) than ingenuine people.

The review of the literature pertaining to the teacher's classroom congruence or genuineness confirms the fact that this construct has not been investigated sufficiently even though it is felt to be an important teacher characteristic.

Congruence in a Classroom Interaction

When we are authentic with another person, we present ourselves as we really are. That is, we face our inner feelings and make them available to the other person as honestly as possible. This condition of interpersonal relations is called congruence or genuineness. Again, the classroom operation of this characteristic is illustrated in the following example:

Student (A Negro):   I don't think you like blacks.

Teacher: You may be right. I want to examine my attitudes and try to eliminate the prejudiced ones, but my deepest feeling is that you don't think I like *you*.

Student: That's right. I don't think any of us blacks is as important as the white students. You're always calling us by the wrong names and you don't make that mistake with the white students.

Teacher: I can only apologize for times when I've done that, but since I also make that mistake with white students, I feel like you're singling out things which prove your point.

Student: You use high-sounding words about liking others, but you're a fraud.

Teacher: You mean I'm not perfect.

Student: If you're going to talk about something, you ought to be able to do it.

Teacher: That doesn't leave me much of a starting point. You see, if I'm to improve as a person, I've got to be able to grow, too. You don't seem to want to give me that right. You make me feel very bad and it seems to me you *want* to, at this point.

Student: You're a Ph.D. and you're supposed to be something special . . . you should know better than to be prejudiced.

Teacher: You've avoided the issue of my feelings about you. There are times when I don't like you because you seem to want to embarrass others. I don't like that from blacks or whites.

Student: As smart as you're supposed to be that shouldn't bother you.

Teacher: Teachers are supposed to be immune to their feelings? I hope I never am. But you've failed to come to grips with *your* feelings. It seems to me you want me to dislike you—then you're safe in disliking me.

Student: I get along well with white people. I like most of them. . .I don't think there's anything different about blacks.

Teacher: I agree there's nothing intrinsically different about blacks, but there are conditions which blacks face in some communities which whites don't have to face, and it seems to me that makes you angry. It makes me angry, too, but I'd be angrier if I were black.

Student: You're not angry. You're like all the rest. You just talk good.

Teacher: I think I am different and that creates conflict in you. I don't fit into your categories. You're having a hard time writing me off as just another white man.

Student: You don't understand.

Teacher: Maybe I don't, but I want to.

Student: I don't think you can.

Teacher:	That's a good excuse for not trying.
Student:	I don't think it's worth trying.
Teacher:	You don't think *it's* worth it or *I'm* worth it?
Student:	You won't make it.
Teacher:	Those are your words, not mine.
Student:	Why don't we talk about it later?
Teacher:	Good, I'll see you tomorrow.

The incident might have proceeded differently:

Student (Negro):	I don't think you like blacks.
Teacher:	I don't see how you can feel that way after all the things I've done for you.
Student:	You just help me because I'm a black. You're trying to look good.
Teacher:	You're not helping your race by talking like that. The other blacks seem to like me. Maybe it's that we just have some communication problems.
Student:	Yeah, I'm sure we have communication problems.
Teacher:	You know, it often takes students a while to get used to the way I joke and kid. You'll understand me better as the term goes along.
Student:	Yeah, maybe.

The teacher failed to confront his feelings about the student and placed the student in a defensive position with every response. The issue was not sharply defined.

The first confrontation between teacher and student did not resolve the conflict, but it placed the issue squarely before them. The student's attack on the teacher may have been justified, but his (the teacher's) feelings about the situation and the student were communicated to the student who was in turn confronted with his feelings. Perhaps the relationship is unresolvable, but a denial of its existence only buries it deeper where its effect is even more devastating. One of the most common obstacles to genuine relationships between teacher and student is the feeling that the teacher should like all his students, and this leads inexorably to internal conflict between one's real self and one's ideal self. Only the ideal self likes all the students. Our real self reacts negatively to the destructive acts of students and we communicate these feelings to students whether or not we verbalize them. They are resolvable only when they are faced openly and mutually.

72

Measuring a Teacher's Genuineness

Using the In-Service Training Scale

The Rogerian term applied to "being one's self in a human relationship" is congruence. This is a little esoteric, so we selected a more commonly used word, genuineness, as a label for our in-service training scale for measuring that dimension. The in-service scale for genuineness is designed to communicate that most school teachers assume a role while they teach, and their relationship to students is limited by their role. As a result they do not relate to their students as "real" people. While it is relatively easy to spot a phony, it is a bit more difficult to discriminate between a teacher who is being himself and one who is playing a role, because most of us expect teachers to act like "school teachers." Therefore, the poles for the scale evolved from two different kinds of teacher behavior, namely "school teacher's voice" and spontaneous, normal conversation. The former is considered low-genuine behavior while the latter is referred to as high-genuine behavior.

The training procedures for the scale are as follows:

1. A trainer makes a didactic presentation explaining genuineness and the scale.
2. The group listens to standard audio tape recordings of classroom teaching and assigns ratings according to the scale. This procedure is continued until the trainer is convinced that the trainees understand the dimension and the scale.
3. The group divides into small groups (4 or 5) and volunteers bring audio tape recordings of their teaching to be evaluated by the group. This continues as long as it appears productive for the group members.

Since understanding the dimension is the chief goal of this in-service training scale, precision as to reliability is relatively unimportant at this stage.

In-Service Training Scale: Teacher's Genuineness in Classroom Interaction

Level 1
All of the teacher's verbal communications are ritualistic. They seem to be mechanical or practiced.
Example: (1) The teacher sounds like a "school teacher" in voice and manner.

(2) The teacher slowly and/or mechanically says, "Turn to page 99 and begin reading silently."

Level 2
Most of the teacher's verbal communications are ritualistic, but a few are somewhat spontaneous.

Example: (1) The teacher sounds like a "school teacher" most of the time, but occasionally she sounds as if she is having a "normal" conversation.

(2) The teacher rather slowly says, "Turn to page 99 and begin reading silently," but she gives evidence of some (though not much) vitality.

Level 3
The teacher's verbal communications are about equally distributed between ritualistic and spontaneous.

Example: (1) The teacher sounds like a "school teacher" about half the time, while for the other half she seems to be having a "normal" conversation.

(2) The teacher says, "Let's turn to page 99 and begin reading," and she gives evidence of normal vitality. She is neither wildly enthusiastic nor dull.

Level 4
Most of the teacher's verbal communications are spontaneous, but a few are ritualistic.

Example: (1) The teacher only rarely sounds like a "school teacher." Most of the time she sounds as though she is engaging in "normal" conversation.

(2) The teacher says, "Hey, let's turn to page 99, and would anyone like to read to us?"

Level 5
All of the teacher's verbal communications are spontaneous. They are neither mechanical nor practiced.

Example: (1) The teacher always sounds as if she is having "normal" conversation.

(2) The teacher says, "What do you want to read today? Does anyone know an exciting story?"

Using the Carkhuff Scale for Facilitative Genuineness
The Carkhuff Scale is more detailed and precise than the in-service training scale, and, therefore, requires more preparation. Again, training

74

in the discrimination and communication of interpersonal dimensions is the most effective vehicle for making accurate ratings.[7]

Precision is a concern of the Carkhuff Scale and inter-rater and intra-rater reliabilities are important. Since the usual rating procedure involves three raters working independently, it is important that they are trained effectively and, also, that they stay in communication with each other as they continue to rate. This latter step insures an on-going in-service program for the raters.

Carkhuff Scale: Facilitative Genuineness in Interpersonal Processes*

Level 1

The first person's verbalizations are clearly unrelated to what he is feeling at the moment, or his only genuine responses are negative in regard to the second person(s) and appear to have a totally destructive effect upon the second person.

Example: The first person may be defensive in his interaction with the second person(s) and this defensiveness may be demonstrated in the content of his words or his voice quality and where he is defensive he does not employ his reaction as a basis for potentially valuable inquiry into the relationship.

In summary, there is evidence of a considerable discrepancy between the first person's inner experiencing and his current verbalizations, or where there is no discrepancy, the first person's reactions are employed solely in a destructive fashion.

Level 2

The first person's verbalizations are slightly unrelated to what he is feeling at the moment or when his responses are genuine they are negative in regard to the second person and the first person does not appear to know how to employ his negative reactions constructively as a basis for inquiry into the relationship.

---

*The present scale, "Facilitative Genuineness in Interpersonal Processes" has been derived in part from "A Tentative Scale for the Measurement of Therapist Genuineness of Self-Congruence" by C. B. Truax which has been validated in extensive process and outcome research on counseling and psychotherapy (summarized in Truax and Carkhuff[8]) and in part from an earlier version which has been similarly validated (summarized in Carkhuff and Berenson[9]). In addition, similar measures of similar constructs have received support in the literature of counseling and therapy and education. The present scale was written to apply to all interpersonal processes and represents a systematic attempt to reduce the ambiguity and increase the reliability of the scale. In the process, many important delineations and additions have been made. For comparative purposes, the levels of the present scale are approximately equal to the stages of the earlier scale, although the systematic emphasis upon the constructive employment of negative reactions represents a pronounced divergence of emphasis.[10]

Example: The first person may respond to the second person(s) in a professional manner that has a rehearsed quality or quality concerning the way a helper "should" respond in that situation.

In summary, the first person is usually responding according to his prescribed role rather than to express what he personally feels or means and when he is genuine his responses are negative and he is unable to employ them as a basis for further inquiry.

Level 3

The first person provides no "negative" cues between what he says and what he feels, but he provides no positive cues to indicate a really genuine response to the second person(s).

Example: The first person may listen and follow the second person(s) but commits nothing more of himself.

In summary, the first person appears to make appropriate responses which do not seem insincere but which do not reflect any real involvement either. Level 3 constitutes the minimal level of facilitative interpersonal functioning.

Level 4

The facilitator presents some positive cues indicating a genuine response (whether positive or negative) in a non-destructive manner to the second person(s).

Example: The facilitator's expressions are congruent with his feelings although he may be somewhat hesitant about expressing them fully.

In summary, the facilitator responds with many of his own feelings and there is no doubt as to whether he really means what he says and he is able to employ his responses whatever the emotional content, as a basis for further inquiry into the relationship.

Level 5

The facilitator is freely and deeply himself in a non-exploitative relationship with the second person(s).

Example: The facilitator is completely spontaneous in his interaction and open to experiences of all types, both pleasant and hurtful; and in the event of hurtful responses the facilitator's comments are employed constructively to open a further area of inquiry for both the facilitator and the second person.

In summary, the facilitator is clearly being himself and yet employing his own genuine responses constructively.

The Relationship of Teacher Genuineness to Classroom Interaction

One of the major questions in education involves the identification of behaviors which are characteristic of specific dimensions of the classroom climate. At this junction it is possible to use data from Interaction Analysis such as those of Flanders[11] to investigate the relationship between specific behaviors and the ratings for the Genuineness Scale. One essential question is that of the interaction patterns of relatively genuine teachers as compared to relatively ungenuine ones.

To complete this study the audio tape recordings of twenty-five "high genuine" teachers (3.0 and above) were evaluated by the Flanders' Interaction Analysis and compared to the same analysis of twenty-five "low genuine" teachers (2.0 and below). The population included five teachers from each grade level 1-5 and all were female. Since this was essentially a descriptive investigation, no other controls were used.

Results

The ratings for genuineness were completed by three raters according to the procedures described earlier. The means for both groups of teachers by grade level are displayed in Table 1. The t-statistic obtained for the

Table 1

Mean "Genuineness" Ratings of Teachers
by Grade Levels and Groups

Grade Level	Mean "Genuineness" Ratings of Teachers					
	"Low Genuine" Teachers			"High Genuine" Teachers		
	N	$\overline{X}$	o^2	N	$\overline{X}$	o^2
1	5	1.66	.3180	5	3.28	.0770
2	5	1.46	.2080	5	3.32	.0370
3	5	2.00	.0000	5	3.38	.1020
4	5	1.80	.2000	5	3.20	.0670
5	5	1.96	.0080	5	3.30	.1100
Totals	25	1.78	.0098	25	3.31	.0003

difference between the means of the total groups was significant beyond the .001 level (calculated $t = 15.996530$).

Two ANOVA's (shown in Table 2) were carried out to test the hypothesis of no significant contribution to the variance of the genuineness conditions by grade level. Both yielded F-ratios which were not significant.

The Flanders' Interaction Analyses were done by two additional (independent) raters who had used it extensively in other studies. The results are displayed in Table 3.

The results indicate that the "high genuine" teachers use significantly more praise, significantly less criticism, and elicit significantly more student initiated talk, while their classrooms have about the same amount of silence or confusion.

Table 2

Equivalences Between Grade Level Means
Within "High" and "Low" Genuine Conditions

Source	Low Genuine Conditions				High Genuine Conditions			
	DF	SS	MS	F	DF	SS	MS	F
Among	4	.9896	.2474	1.6852*	4	.0344	.0086	.1094
Within	20	2.9360	.1468		20	1.5720	.0786	
Total	24	3.9256			24	1.6064		

$*.95F_{4,24} = 2.78$

Conclusion

The data indicate that it is possible to train raters to reliably employ a scale designed to measure teacher genuineness. The ratings from the scale relate to data from Flanders' Interaction Analysis in the expected directions. That is, "high genuine" teachers when compared to "low genuine" teachers employ significantly more praise, significantly less criticism, and obtain significantly more student-initiated responses. All these differences may be described as being characteristic of teachers who are student-centered.

Table 3

Differential Patterns of "High" and "Low" Genuine Teachers When Analyzed for Flanders' Interaction Categories

| Flanders' Categories | Mean No. of Behaviors in Category | | | |
	High Genuine Teachers (N=25)	Low Genuine Teachers (N=25)	t-statistic	Level of Significance
1. Accepts Feelings	.40	.16	1.500	NS
2. Praises	8.67	2.76	4.232	.001
3. Uses Student Ideas	19.32	13.20	1.716	NS
4. Asks Questions	36.56	29.78	1.107	NS
5. Lectures	30.28	46.12	1.383	NS
6. Gives Directions	17.92	13.16	1.105	NS
7. Criticizes	2.96	7.80	-2.264	.05
8. Student Responds	72.40	101.16	-2.408	.02
9. Student Initiates	40.92	7.00	5.585	.001
10. Silence or Confusion	11.04	17.68	-1.589	NS

Summary

This chapter presents a scale for the measurement of teacher genuineness, an interpersonal process variable similar to the characteristic called congruence by Carl Rogers.[12] The scale and the procedure for using it are described and the results from one study are reported. The investigation compared data from the use of the Genuineness Scale to data for the same teachers from Flanders' Interaction Analysis with the general finding that teacher genuineness is positively related to characteristics commonly associated with student-centered behaviors. These results are to be expected, but they raise another question: Is a teacher genuine because she is student centered or vice versa? This question has rather great implications for teacher training since it raises the issue of whether to enhance teacher genuineness by working with attitudinal dimensions or by teaching specific behaviors. This study indicates that there is a tendency for "high" genuine teachers to behave differently from "low" genuine ones and this is important since previous research has demonstrated that teacher genuineness is related both to improved cognitive gain and to self-concept enhancement among students.[13,14,15] This study presents a procedure through which this issue can be explored.

1. Building a classroom climate for learning. *NEA Journal,* December, 1961, *50,* 34-8.

2. Stephens, J. M. *The psychology of classroom learning.* New York: Holt, Rinehart and Winston, 1965.

3. Bowers, R. E. and Soar, R. S. Influence of teacher personality on classroom interaction. *Journal of Experimental Education,* June, 1962, *30,* 309-11.

4. Thurman, H. Putting yourself in another's place. *Childhood Education,* February, 1962, *38,* 259-60.

5. Stansfield, R. N. Human side of teaching. *Peabody Journal of Education,* May, 1961, *38,* 345-50.

6. Bills, R. E. Helpful people. Mimeographed paper presented to Kentucky ASCD, October, 1964.

7. Carkhuff, R. R. *Helping and human relations: A primer for lay and professional helpers. Vol. I. Selection and training. Vol. II. Practice and research.* New York: Holt, Rinehart and Winston, 1969.

8. Truax, C. B. and Carkhuff, R. R. *Toward effective counseling and psychotherapy.* Chicago: Aldine, 1967.

9. Carkhuff, R. R. and Berenson, B. *Beyond counseling and therapy.* New York: Holt, Rinehart and Winston, 1968.

10. Carkhuff, *op. cit.*

11. Flanders, N. A. Teacher influence on pupil attitudes and achievement. U. S. Department of Health, Education and Welfare, Cooperative Research Monograph No. 12. Washington, D. C.: Government Printing Office, 1965.

12. Rogers, C. R. *On becoming a person.* Boston: Houghton-Mifflin Co., 1961. P. 287.

13. Jourard, S. M. *The transparent self: Self-disclosure and well-being.* Princeton, N.J.: Van Nostrand Co., Inc. 1964.

14. Spaulding, R.L. *Achievement, creativity, and self-concept correlates of teacher-pupil transactions in elementary schools.* U.S. Office of Education, Cooperative Research Report No. 1352. Urbana: University of Illinois, 1963.

15. Aspy, D. N. The effects of teacher-offered conditions of empathy, positive regard, and congruence upon student achievement. *Florida Journal of Educational Research,* 1969, *11* (1), 39-48.

Positive Regard: 6
IN HUMANE CLASSROOMS
TEACHERS VALUE THEIR STUDENTS

The use of positive regard as a construct in educational research is limited mainly to those investigators implementing the theoretical models of Carl Rogers.[1] However, the term is closely allied with warmth, a term used rather widely by other researchers, so the review of literature will cite some studies investigating warmth.

Cronbach affirms the importance of warmth. He comments, "In studies of teacher success, warmth consistently appears as one of the two most important qualities (orderliness being the other)." But he cautions that the definition of warmth is not precise and lists five general definitions as follows:

1. Spontaneous expression of feeling. The teacher colors classroom relationships with a continual expression of his own enthusiasm and liking for his pupils.
2. Support and encouragement. Reinforcement is contingent; teacher approves of the pupil as a person, his goal, and helps him over obstacles.
3. Contingent social reinforcement. The teacher gives plentiful praise, but only when he judges the pupil's actions to be meritorious. Approval is given when it is earned, not otherwise.
4. Tact and consideration. Criticism or rejection of a pupil's proposal is presented in such a way that the pupil does not feel blamed or inferior.
5. Acceptance of pupil's feelings. The teacher encourages the pupil to express his interests, fears, etc., and takes them seriously.[2]

He assesses the present state of research of warmth in the classroom in this manner: "Each investigation defines warmth in a different way, and few studies carry us beyond the obvious finding that considerateness is better than harshness."[3]

Soar's findings caution against underestimating the importance of students' attitudes toward teachers:

> In classrooms in which students have more desirable attitudes toward their teacher and schoolwork the students also have a greater opportunity to express their own ideas and feelings and the teacher tends more often to ask questions, to work with ideas suggested by students, to praise or encourage student action, and to accept and clarify feeling tone in a non-threatening manner. In those classrooms in which attitudes are less desirable, the teacher spends more of his time lecturing and ... gives more directions and criticism.[4]

The conditions concomitant with favorable attitudes seem to be generally conducive to learning, so, perhaps, the favorable attitude is a basic ingredient of the "good" learning climate.

Cogan found that, "Warm, considerate teachers get an unusual amount of original poetry and art from children."[5]

McKeachie investigated the relation of teacher warmth to student achievement and made this observation:

> Warmth, as rated by students and observers, relates to achievement differently for men and women and for students high and low in need affiliation. If warmth affects some students positively and others negatively, the effect may cancel out in a simple correlational study.[6]

Christenson's studies of teacher warmth and achievement growth of fourth graders found the following:

> ... results support the contention that affective response of the teacher is more important for growth in achievement than permissiveness.[7]

Reed investigated teacher warmth and pupils' interest using thirty-eight general science teachers and 1,045 ninth grade students. He found a correlation of .20 for boys and .28 for girls, significant at the .001 level. His conclusions were as follows:

1. It appears valid to state with considerable confidence this generalization concerning the relationship between pupils' perceptions of teachers' behavior that relax interpersonal tensions (warmth) and pupil change criteria: when the criteria are comprehensive and/or attitudinal in nature, the correlation will be significant, positive, and of moderate strength.
2. It appears plausible to state a second more tentative generalization concerning the relationship between teacher

warmth and pupil change criteria: when the criteria are informational in nature and are school goals that are rewarded by the marking system, there will be low correlations or a negative relationship. *For criteria of this nature, one would predict that the direction of effect of teacher warmth will change from positive to zero or negative as the pupil age increases.*[8]

Smith's findings from investigations of the interaction in secondary classrooms may indicate the basic reason that the significance of the classroom climate decreases with age:

In my studies of teaching I find that over 70% of verbal behavior in the classroom is concerned with cognition, with understanding the terms, principles, facts, etc., of the fields of instruction. About 12% is concerned with classroom mechanics and the like, and the rest (18%) is by way of reinforcement and encouragement.[9]

It is significant that Smith is not differentiating between good and bad practice, but rather enumerating what occurs. It may be that one impediment to learning is the small percentage (18%) of affective content in the teacher-pupil relationship.

Reed reports two studies which confirm the inverse relationship of age and significance of teacher warmth. In the first, Brookover found a negative relationship (r=-.22) between eleventh grade pupils' rating of the warmth of teacher-pupil relationship and the informational gains in United States history. The second by McCall found that sixth grade pupils' judgments of teachers' kindness was one moderately strong predictor of pupil growth.[10]

Brown's study of third graders' reading improvement, as measured by pre- and post-test performance on the Stanford Achievement test, indicated the following:

Teacher responses which were (1) learner supportive statements or questions, (2) acceptant or clarifying statements or questions, and (3) problem structuring statements or questions, related to significant student improvement on the arithmetic section of the test. This was true only for overachievers and underachievers.[11]

Brown investigated reading improvement because "reading is one of the most crucial skills, if not the most crucial skill, for successful achievement in most areas of the elementary school curriculum."[12]

Brown's investigation employed observer reports of the classroom interaction, and, while this is a dynamic evaluation of the process, it is limited by the inability to check intra-judge ratings for a specific incident.

Della Piana and Gage report these findings: "Pupils who were achievement-oriented were concerned with how well the teacher explained and helped them learn. These pupils ratings of teachers correlated only .20 with the teacher's warmth and sympathy."[13] This is consistent with other research that indicates the relationship of pupils' needs to their reaction to the teacher's characteristics. It may also be consistent with the hypothesis that the significance of teacher warmth decreases with pupil age if achievement orientation is a more advanced developmental stage than need for warmth.

Travers, who emphasizes learning theory in much of his writing, speaks of warmth as a reinforcer:

> The warm, approving type of behavior on the part of the teacher, which was recommended by the progressive education movement, is the focus of this concept (permissive classrooms). It is clearly reinforcing, though the progressives did not fully appreciate the reinforcements provided by the social role of the teacher.[14]

This view appears to corroborate the contention that warmth is a factor in the learning process since positive reinforcement has been demonstrated to improve learning rates.

Prescott may have expressed the experiential component of love or warmth when he says:

> The effective teacher will have active and sincere valuing of each child at all times . . . when the teacher listens to and accepts what he has to say, when he can feel some warmth in the relationship, then he feels deep inside that he is valued, that he has a friend.[15]

It seems significant to include Prescott's description of the place of love in the classroom:

> It was not until I had analyzed the nature of love that I realized that love has a place in the classroom and that genuine love is neither romantic nor instinctive. It is a valuing to the degree that one achieves empathy with the loved one and a willingness to make one's resources available to promote his self-realization. Many teachers satisfy these criteria of love for particular children who are insecure and have great need of it.[16]

This holds that love is not important to all students—only those who do not receive sufficient amounts elsewhere.

Stephens asserts a similar need for some students: "A warm, accepting attitude is especially important for pupils who have already come to think of the world as hostile, critical, and unaccepting."[17]

Menninger adds his voice to this position: "Among the basic

requirements for healthy development of personality probably the most difficult lesson that every child needs to learn is how to love and be loved."[18]

Stabler presents experiential evidence to support the place of love in the classroom for problem children and offers the following hypothesis: "Perhaps one reason why failure is experienced in helping 'problem children' is because teachers cannot honestly say, 'I love those boys.' "[19]

The literature related to unconditional positive regard and its impact upon learning refers most frequently to teacher warmth or love. This does not appear to be a retreat from the issue since Rogers says that positive regard "means a kind of love for the person as he is, providing we understand the word love as equivalent to the theologian's term 'agape,' and not in its usual romantic and possessive meanings."[20]

There appears to be consensus that (1) the definition of warmth is not precise, (2) students respond differentially to warmth, (3) the effect of warmth upon student achievement is not clearly defined, and (4) there is a need to investigate the effect of warmth upon students.

Positive Regard in the Classroom Interaction

When we value another person and relate to them in such a way that we demonstrate the conviction that they deserve all the things characteristic of a "good life," we have positive regard for that person. This kind of valuing transcends the more commonly used terms such as warmth or caring, and, since it is based on a deep conviction, it is not a *technique* for building "good" relationships. It is not something we *use*. It is something we *are*, or it does not exist.

The following example illustrates a teacher's communication of his positive regard:

Student: (Sobs in a release of tension.) I just can't take the final tomorrow.

Teacher: Would you like to share your problem with me?

Student: It's a long story. (Sobs.)

Teacher: I have time, and I'd like to be helpful.

Student: This has been a rough term . . . . The family has had all kinds of problems. Mother and Dad separated and my younger sister has been *really* hurt. She's been right in the middle of the whole mess. (Sobs.)

Teacher:	It hurts a lot when our loved ones suffer, particularly children.
Student:	I got so I didn't want to go home and hear all the bickering going on. They all wanted me to take their side.
Teacher:	You must be a good person to talk to.
Student:	Maybe, but my parents just wanted to get me to take their side. My sister was different. She really needed someone to talk to.
Teacher:	You were about the only constructive person she could turn to. She trusted you and felt like you understood.
Student:	I guess so, but things got a lot worse. (Sobs violently.)
Teacher:	(Holds student's hands.) It's O.K. Let it all out.
Student:	(She calms and sits quietly for some time.)
Teacher:	(After student seems more composed.) Sometimes a good cry eases some of the hurt.
Student:	I wish my mother had cried . . . . Maybe she'd still be alive. (Pauses.) She shot herself last week.
Teacher:	I've lost my mother, too. I know it takes a lot of courage to face that loss. You've been through some hard knocks which make some of us feel like giving up . . . .
Student:	Yeah. I guess that's what Mom did. The separation really hit her hard.
Teacher:	I guess we wonder if the same thing might happen to us—whether we have the courage to see our own situation through.
Student:	Yeah. I want to live, but I just can't take care of everything at once.
Teacher:	Well, you know your *being* is more important to me than anything you do at this time. As far as the exam is concerned we can handle that several different ways. Is there any way you'd prefer?
Student:	I want to take the exam. I wouldn't feel right if I didn't. Would it be possible to postpone it for a few weeks?
Teacher:	Sure. There's no sweat about that.
Student:	Thanks. I feel a lot better.
Teacher:	Good. I wonder if there are some other ways I can be helpful?
Student:	I don't think so right now. The other things will just take time, I guess.
Teacher:	I'm very sorry about your hurt and I want you to know that I've enjoyed knowing you this term and that I'm always interested in your progress.

Student:	Thanks. Maybe I'll come back again just to talk.

An alternative approach might have gone like this:

Student:	(Sobs in release of tension.) I just can't take the final tomorrow.
Teacher:	That's a pretty serious problem. You know the school has policies about that. It takes a specific excuse before the school can make an exception. Do you have one?
Student:	Well, sorta . . . . There's been a lot of trouble in the family.
Teacher:	(Jokingly.) Well, if you can produce a dead body, they might say O.K.
Student:	(Stares silently.) I guess I'll try to take it.
Teacher:	Good luck. It's a tough one. The dean says we've been giving too many A's.

The student who is using all her resources to cope with extra-school problems needs more than relief from her school assignments. She needs an affirmation of her being and a level of caring which frees her to try again.

Measuring a Teacher's Respect for Students

Using the In-Service Training Scale

Although Carl Rogers employed the term unconditional positive regard, we feel it meaningful to use a slightly different word. It seems that even though we have a variety of concepts related to the general area of positive regard, i.e., caring, warmth, valuing, they tend to be associated with weakness. For this reason we have favored the term respect, which connotes the same general notion as positive regard, but tends to evoke more of an idea of strength.

The in-service scale for teacher respect is designed to show that a teacher demonstrates her amount of valuing a student by the degree to which she communicates to him that he is able to use his highest cognitive ability, namely, thinking. Thus, there are two components to this type of respect. The *first* is a belief in the other person's highest abilities, and the *second* is providing tasks which permit him to use them.

The training procedures for the scale are as follows:

1. A trainee makes a didactic presentation explaining the dimension and the scale.

2. The group listens to standard audio tape recordings of classroom teaching and assigns a rating according to the scale. This procedure is continued until the trainer is convinced that the trainees understand the dimension and the scale.
3. The group divides into small groups (4 or 5) and volunteers bring audio tape recordings of their teaching to be evaluated by the group. This continues as long as it appears productive for the group members.

Since understanding the dimension is the goal of this in-service training scale, precision or reliability is relatively unimportant at this stage.

In-Service Training Scale: Teacher's Respect for Students

Level 1
The teacher communicates a *clearly negative* regard for the students' individual abilities to learn.

Examples: (1) The teacher structures the situation so the student takes little or no active part in the learning process; i.e., lectures or gives unnecessarily detailed, repetitive directions, etc.

(2) The teacher seems to mean it when she ways, "I don't expect you to learn this. It's too difficult for you."

Level 2
The teacher communicates a *somewhat negative* regard for the students' individual abilities to operate effectively in learning situations involving memory and recognition (Level 1 of Bloom's Taxonomy, 1967).

Examples: (1) The teacher structures the learning situation so that the student can appropriately respond only by rote, but often fails to allow enough time for even that response; i.e., answers own questions or calls on other students or the class to "help" with the answer. The teacher communicates doubt that the students will be able to participate "correctly."

(2) The teacher says, "Even this is too difficult for many of you."

Level 3
The teacher consistently communicates a *positive* regard for the students' individual abilities to operate effectively in learning situations involving memory and recognition (Level 1 of Bloom's Taxonomy), but

not with the higher intellective processes; i.e., creativity, problem-solving, judgment.

Examples: (1) The teacher structures the situation in such a manner that the students are expected and encouraged to respond at Level 1 of the cognitive processes, but responses at higher levels are not appropriate.

(2) The teacher says, "I'll do the thinking. You pay attention and learn."

Level 4

The teacher consistently communicates a *positive* regard for the students' abilities to operate effectively in learning situations involving memory and recognition (Level 1 of Bloom's Taxonomy), and occasionally allows the students to explore the higher intellective processes.

Examples: (1) The teacher sometimes structures the situation so that she expects responses at higher levels. They are considered appropriate and are received by the teacher as worthwhile contributions to the learning process.

(2) The teacher says, "Let's not strain our brains, but take some time to think of some new ways to do that."

Level 5

The teacher consistently communicates a *positive* regard for the students' abilities to operate effectively at all intellective levels.

Examples: (1) The teacher structures the learning situation so that she expects responses at higher levels. They are always appropriate and encouraged. Such responses are received by the teacher as worthwhile contributions to the learning process.

(2) The teacher says, "I'll bet we can think of a hundred new ways to do that."

Using the Carkhuff Scale for Respect

The Carkhuff Scale is more detailed and precise than the in-service training scale, and, therefore, requires more preparation. Since teachers have a limited amount of time for training, it has been found that utilizing the in-service training scale provides an effective and appropriate transition to training models developed by Carkhuff. Training in the communication of interpersonal skills itself is, of course, the most effective vehicle for learning to discriminate the various dimensions and levels of helping.[21]

Again, precision is a concern of the Carkhuff Scale and inter-rater and intra-rater reliabilities are important. Since the usual rating procedure involves three raters working independently, it is important that they are trained effectively and, also, that they stay in communication with each other as they continue to rate. The latter step insures an on-going in-service training program for the raters.

Carkhuff Scale: Communication of Respect in Interpersonal Processes.*

Level 1
The verbal and behavioral expressions of the first person communicate a clear lack of respect (or negative regard) for the second person(s).
Example: The first person communicates to the second person that the second person's feelings and experiences are not worthy of consideration or that the second person is not capable of acting constructively. The first person may become the sole focus of evaluation.
In summary, in many ways the first person communicates a total lack of respect for the feelings, experiences, and potentials of the second person.

Level 2
The first person responds to the second person in such a way as to communicate little respect for the feelings, experiences, and potentials of the second person.
Example: The first person may respond mechanically or passively or ignore many of the feelings of the second person.
In summary, in many ways the first person displays a lack of respect or concern for the second person's feelings, experiences, and potentials.

---

*The present scale, "Respect or Positive Regard in Interpersonal Processes," has been derived in part from a tentative scale by C.B. Truax which has been validated in extensive process and outcome research on counseling and psychotherapy (summarized in Truax and Carkhuff[22]) and in part from an earlier version which was also validated in extensive process and outcome research on counseling and psychotherapy (summarized in Carkhuff and Berenson[23]). In addition, similar measures of similar constructs have received extensive support in the literature of counseling and therapy and education. The present scale was written to reduce the ambiguity and increase the reliability of the scale. In the process many important delineations and additions have been made. For comparative purposes, the levels of the present scale are approximately equal to the stages of both the earlier scales, although the systematic emphasis upon the positive regard rather than upon unconditionality represents a pronounced divergence of emphasis and the systematic de-emphasis of concern for advice-giving and directionality, both of which may or may not communicate high levels as well as low levels of respect.[24]

90

Level 3

The first person communicates a positive respect and concern for the second person's feelings, experiences, and potentials.

Example: The first person communicates respect and concern for the second person's ability to express himself and to deal constructively with his life situation.

In summary, in many ways the first person communicates that who the second person is and what he does matters to the first person. Level 3 constitutes the minimal level of facilitative interpersonal functioning.

Level 4

The facilitator clearly communicates a very deep respect and concern for the second person.

Example: The facilitator's responses enable the second person to feel free to be himself and to experience being values as an individual.

In summary, the facilitator communicates a very deep caring for the feelings, experiences, and potentials of the second person.

Level 5

The facilitator communicates the very deepest respect for the second person's worth as a person and his potentials as a free individual.

Example: The facilitator cares very deeply for human potentials of the second person.

In summary, the facilitator is committed to the value of the other person as a human being.

The Relationship of Teacher Respect to Classroom Interaction*

In investigating the question of differential patterns of interaction between teachers differing in the levels of respect which they provide in the classroom, one hour of audio tape recordings of normal classroom instruction by twenty-five "high respect" teachers (ratings on the Respect Scale of 3.3 and above) were subjected to Flanders' Interaction Analysis and compared to the same analysis for twenty-five "low respect" teachers (ratings of 2.5 and below). The population included

---

*Abridged from: D. N. Aspy, B. Black, and F. Roebuck, The relationship of teacher-offered conditions of respect to behavior described by Flanders' interaction analysis. *Journal of Negro Education*, Fall, 1972, in press.

five teachers from each grade level 1-5 and all were female. Since this was essentially a descriptive investigation, no other controls were employed.

Results

The ratings for respect were completed by three raters according to the procedures described earlier. The means for both groups of teachers by grade level are displayed in Table 1. The t-statistic obtained for the difference between the means of the total groups was significant beyond the .001 level (calculated $t = 12.89133$).

Two ANOVA's (shown in Table 2) were carried out to test the hypotheses of no significant contribution to the variance of the respect conditions by grade level. Both yielded F-ratios which were not significant.

The Flanders' Interaction Analyses were done by two additional (independent) raters who had used it extensively in other studies. The results are displayed in Table 3.

The data indicate that the "high respect" teachers use significantly more praise or encouragement, more often accept the feelings of students, and use less criticism. Additionally they elicit more student-initiated talk and have fewer instances of silence or confusion during instructional situations.

Table 1

Mean "Respect" Ratings of Teachers by
Grade Levels and Groups

| Grade Level | Mean "Respect" Ratings of Teachers | | | | | |
| | "Low Respect" Teachers | | | "High Respect" Teachers | | |
	N	$\bar{X}$	o^2	N	$\bar{X}$	o^2
1	5	2.08	.0670	5	3.58	.2720
2	5	2.30	.0250	5	3.52	.0770
3	5	1.96	.1330	5	3.68	.2520
4	5	2.10	.3850	5	3.50	.0850
5	5	2.48	.0020	5	3.72	.2770
Totals	25	2.18	.1349	25	3.60	.1683

Table 2

Equivalences Between Grade Level Means
Within "High" and "Low" Respect Conditions

Source	High Respect Conditions				Low Respect Conditions			
	DF	SS	MS	F-ratio	DF	SS	MS	F-ratio
Among	4	.1880	.0470	.2440*	4	.8456	.2114	1.7271*
Within	20	3.8520	.1926		20	2.4480	.1224	
Total	24	4.0400			24	3.2936		

*$.95^F 4,24=2.78$

Table 3

Differential Patterns of "High" and "Low" Respect Teachers
When Analyzed for Flanders' Interaction Categories

Flanders' Categories	Mean No. of Behaviors in Category		t-statistic	Level of Significance
	High Respect Teachers (N=25)	Low Respect Teachers (N=25)		
1. Accepts Feeling	.32	.08	2.201	.05
2. Praises	8.16	2.92	3.267	.01
3. Uses Student Ideas	16.44	15.52	.268	NS
4. Asks Question	32.96	29.68	.570	NS
5. Lectures	31.76	38.80	.613	NS
6. Gives Directions	17.16	16.60	.124	NS
7. Criticizes	3.04	8.80	-2.419	.02
8. Student Responds	69.60	93.32	-1.992	NS
9. Student Initiates	49.72	11.04	4.982	.001
10. Silence or Confusion	9.84	21.96	-2.601	.02

Conclusion and Discussion

Results from this study indicate that it is possible to train raters to reliably employ a scale designed to measure the levels of respect offered by teachers to their students. The ratings from the Respect Scale relate to data from Flanders' Interaction Analysis in the expected directions. That is, the measure of the teacher's respect for students is related to specific behaviors (use of praise or encouragement, acceptance of student feelings, and avoidance of criticism) which would seem to enable the student to perceive himself favorably. The larger amounts of student-initiated talk and the fewer instances of silence or confusion in the classrooms of teachers offering high levels of respect may also be indicative of the student's perception of himself as valued and capable. All of these differences may be described as being characteristic of teachers who are student-centered or who are concerned with the "person in the process."

Summary

This article presents a scale for the measurement of teacher-provided levels of respect, an interpersonal process variable similar to the characteristic called positive regard by Carl Rogers. The scale and the procedures for using it are described and the results from a study are reported. The investigation related data from ratings on the Respect Scale to data for the same teachers from Flanders' Interaction Analysis with the general finding that high levels of respect are positively related to characteristics commonly associated with student-centered behaviors.

Implications from the study may be extremely important in view of the questions raised by Soar's (1968) study of the relationships between presage ("before the learning act" teacher characteristics), process, and product (student outcome) variables. Soar observed that . . .

A second implication of these results may be that numbers of characteristics of the teacher as indicated by these presage measures do relate to product changes in ways which the process measures do not reflect. That is, that the presage-product relationships only relatively infrequently can be accounted for by means of the intervening, interrelated process. The implication suggested is that the process measures used here have missed aspects of process to which the pupils in the classroom were responding . . . . There seems little question but that prediction of pupil growth from process measures is more successful than from presage measures, but at the same time it is clear that presage characteristics that relate to pupil change are not consistently reflected in process measures.[25]

It may be that some of the "missed aspects of process to which the pupils . . . were responding" are the more global, interpersonal attitudinal processes such as the teacher's communication of respect for the individual student. This does not seem unreasonable in view of the relationships found between Respect ratings and several of the more specific behaviors measured by the Flanders' Categories whose predictive value have already been established. It would be theoretically valid to expect that this kind of global process measure would more consistently reflect presage characteristics since it is "closer" to those characteristics; i.e., in effect the interpersonal attitudinal process acts as an intervening variable which mediates the more specific behaviors. As such, it should be highly predictive since it would be more stable from situation to situation whereas the specific behaviors are adjusted to meet situational demands. Some support for this hypothesis is indicated by the data in Table 3 in which the category reaching the highest significance level is a student outcome variable. Future studies of the predictive value of the Respect Scale may well demonstrate that "Smile when you say *my* name, podner" is just as good advice for teachers as for gunslingers!

1. Cronbach, L. J. *Educational psychology*. New York: Harcourt, Brace and World, 1963.

2. *Ibid.*

3. *Ibid.*

4. Soar, R. S. Effects of teachers' classroom methods and personality on pupil learning. *High School Journal*, May, 1961, *44*, 288-92.

5. Cogan, M. L. The behavior of teachers and the productive behavior of their pupils. *Journal of Experimental Psychology*, 1958, *27*, 89-124.

6. McKeachie, W. J. Motivation, teaching methods and college learning. Nebraska Symposium on Motivation, Lincoln: University of Nebraska Press, 1961. Pp. 111-146.

7. Christenson, C. M. Relationships between pupil achievement, pupil affect-need, teacher warmth, and teacher permissiveness. *Journal of Educational Psychology,* June, 1960, *51,* 169-74.

8. Reed, H. B. Effects of teacher warmth. *Journal of Teacher Education,* September, 1961, *12,* 330-4.

9. Smith, B. O. Conceptual framework for analysis of classroom social interaction: Comments on four papers. *Journal of Experimental Education.* June, 1962, *30,* 325-6.

10. Reed, *op. cit.,* pp. 330-4.

11. Brown, G. I. Which pupil to which classroom climate? *Elementary School Journal,* February, 1960, *60,* 265-9.

12. *Ibid.*

13. Della Piana, G. M. and Gage, N. L. Pupils' values and validity of the MTAI. *Journal of Educational Psychology,* 1955, *46,* 167-178.

14. Traverse, R. M. *Essentials of learning.* New York: MacMillan, 1963.

15. Prescott, D. The child in the educative process. New York: McGraw-Hill, 1957.

16. *Ibid.*

17. Stephens, J. M. *The psychology of classroom learning.* New York: Holt, Rinehart and Winston, 1965.

18. Menninger, W. C. Mental health in our schools. *Education Leadership,* 1950, *7,* 520.

19. Stabler, E. What is this thing called love? *Peabody Journal of Education,* May, 1960, *37,* 338.

20. Rogers, C. R. *On becoming a person.* Boston: Houghton, Mifflin, 1961.

21. Carkhuff, R. R. *Helping and human relations: A primer for lay and professional helpers. Vol. I. Selection and training. Vol. II. Practice and research.* New York: Holt, Rinehart and Winston, 1969.

22. Truax, C. B. and Carkhuff, R. R. *Toward effective counseling and psychotherapy.* Chicago: Aldine, 1967.

23. Carkhuff, R. R. and Berenson, B. *Beyond counseling and therapy.* New York: Holt, Rinehart and Winston, 1968.

24. Carkhuff, *op cit.*

25. Soar, R. S. The study of presage-process-product relationships: Implications for classroom process measurement. Educational Research Association, Los Angeles, California, February, 1968. Pp. 8-9.

Success Promotion: 7

IN HUMANE CLASSROOMS STUDENTS' GOALS COUNT, TOO.

Student performances are generally enhanced by success and retarded by failure. This assertion seems to represent a point of agreement from many diverse points of view. B. F. Skinner states that, "Not only education but Western culture as a whole is moving away from aversive practices . . . . Not only can aversive practices be replaced, they can be replaced with far more powerful techniques."[1] LaBenne and Greene state the case a bit differently when they hold that:

> It has been said many times before that, "nothing succeeds like success." . . . This axiom can be made operational only when teachers provide meaningful activities in which students can explore and discover the personal meaning of events for themselves. To do this demands that teachers know the students and select for them experiences that provide, at a minimum, the opportunity for success.[2]

Purkey summarizes the research in this area by stating, "Just as poor performance lowers self-regard, successful performance raises it."[3] There seems to be widespread support for the general position that success is an essential ingredient of positive human growth and development.

Definitions of Success

External Criteria
A common definition of success involves the attainment of some externally judged goal. Specifically, in the educational context success has been defined frequently as a student's correct performance as assessed by his teacher. Additionally, there is a host of research employing achievement test scores as measures of student success.

Thus, criteria for school success tend to have two major characteristics: (1) correctness as measured by authorities, and (2) measures of outcomes of some educative process, i.e., differences between pre- and post-test scores.

Internal Criteria

Another definition of success is possible if we move from an external frame of reference to an internal one. A. S. Neill dealt with this issue in his book, *Summerhill*. He wrote: "Of course, the philistine can say, 'Humph, so you call a truck driver a success in life!' My own criterion of success is the ability to work joyfully and to live positively."[4] As reflected in Neill's statement, success, in the internal frame of reference, is a positive feeling about one's current activity. In this sense success becomes a process rather than an outcome, because it is dynamically related to present actions.

Success Promotion

When a teacher acts to promote success as an on-going process within her students, she must attend to and respond to their cues which disclose their directionality. For example, two frequent cues given by students are (1) their questions, and (2) their self-initiated remarks. Therefore, the teacher who wants to promote student success can respond to these cues for her own direction. Success promotion, then, is a process employed by a teacher in which she attends to and uses cues from the students which indicate what they wish to do with class time.

Measuring the Process of Success Promotion

Using the foregoing ideas, the following scale for success promotion was devised.

Level 1
The teacher's verbal behavior is directed *exclusively* toward accomplishing her goals without regard to those of her students.
Examples:　(1)　The teacher ignores the students' questions.
　　　　　　(2)　The teacher punishes student behavior which she deems is away from the lesson. She seems to pursue her pre-established schedule rigidly.

Level 2
The teacher's verbal behavior is directed *primarily* toward

accomplishing her goals, but occasionally she acts to help students achieve their self-selected goals.

Examples: (1) The teacher responds to a few student questions, but ignores most of them.

(2) The teacher occasionally allows a student to discuss something "off the subject." She seems very aware both of being in charge of the group and of covering a prescribed amount of material.

Level 3

The teacher's verbal behavior is directed toward accomplishing her goals about 50% of the time and the students' self-selected goals about 50% of the time.

Examples: (1) The teacher responds to about half of the students' questions.

(2) The teacher gets "off the subject" about 50% of the time in the sense that she enters into a dialogue with students. She seems to feel in charge of the group and concerned about covering a prescribed amount of material. However, she does not seem anxious about it.

Level 4

The teacher's verbal behavior is directed primarily toward helping her students accomplish their self-selected goals, but occasionally she acts to accomplish her goals without regard to those of the students.

Examples: (1) The teacher responds to most of the students' questions.

(2) The teacher "gets off the subject" easily. In fact, she seems to enjoy doing so and sustains it by eliciting a large number of student-initiated statements. She gives only slight evidence of either being in charge or being limited by the amount of material to be covered.

Level 5

All of the teacher's verbal behavior is directed toward helping students accomplish their self-selected goals without regard to her own goals.

Examples: (1) The teacher's approach is geared to cope with all the students' questions as they state them.

(2) The teacher's subject matter consists solely of the process of helping students accomplish their goals. She converses with them freely and openly without any evidence of being limited by either concern for being in charge or the amount of material to be covered.

This scale has been reliably (*r* above .80) applied to six studies and sixteen in-service training programs. It seems to be an effective instrument for teacher training.

The Difference in the Classroom Behaviors of High and Low Promoters of Success

Problem

There is a need to know if teachers who are rated high in promoting success perform differently from those who are rated "low" in success promotion. This is significant for teacher training programs whose thrust is toward producing teachers who facilitate their students' growth by dealing with their internal frames of reference. However, it is also important for all teacher training, and Cronbach summarizes it well when he says, "The moral of these and other studies is that success or hope of success nearly always increases interest and effort."[5] Therefore, if we can identify specific teacher behaviors which are characteristic of this success promotion, then training for those behaviors can be instituted in a teacher training program. On the other hand, there is a need to know if success promotion is an attitudinal variable which is unrelated to specific behaviors and must be taught by other means.

Methodology

Population. The sample included sixty female elementary teachers (ten from each grade level 1-6). Thirty (5 from each grade level) were rated high (3.0 or above) for success promotion, while thirty (5 from each grade level) were rated low (2.3 or below). Twenty-one were Negro while the remainder were white. Twenty-eight had less than five years teaching experience, and the others had five years or more teaching experience. No other controls were employed in the study. All participants were volunteers.

Teaching samples. The teachers were instructed to audio tape record one hour of their normal instruction of reading groups. Four three-minute segments from each hour of teaching were evaluated by raters trained to apply each of the instruments. The segments were selected from (1) the beginning of the hour, (2) about one-third into the hour, (3) two-thirds into the hour, and (4) at the end of hour. Each scale was employed by a different set of raters.

Flanders' Interaction Analysis. Each of the audio tape segments was evaluated according to Flanders' Interaction Analysis by two experienced raters who maintained at least 95% agreement throughout the rating procedure. The scores in the data represent the total number of teacher behaviors which fell in each of the selected Flanders' categories for all four segments.

Carkhuff Scales.[6] The Carkhuff Scales assess levels of Empathy, Congruence, and Positive Regard in an interpersonal interaction. They were applied to each of the segments by three trained raters who maintained intra-rater correlations of .85 while the separate raters maintained an agreement level of 85%. The ratings presented in the data are means for the three raters of all four segments. Thus, each rating presented in the data is the mean of 12 separate ratings.

Success Promotion Scale. The Success Promotion Scale[7] was applied to each of the segments by three raters who maintained an intra-rater (rate, re-rate) correlation of .85. They also maintained an agreement rate of 85%. The scores represent the means of four ratings by three raters. Therefore, each rating in the data is the mean of 12 separate ratings.

Results

Raw scores for each group on each variable were transformed into T-scores. The T-scores for the six measures which previous studies had indicated to be most important in discriminating between high and low groups on success promotion are presented in Table 1 and Figure 1. These measures are:

Flanders categories:	3	Acceptance or use of student ideas,
	7	Criticism, and
	9	Student initiated talk.
Carkhuff Scales:	E	Empathy,
	C	Congruence, and
	PR	Positive Regard.

Discriminant function analysis based on these six variables for sixty subjects correctly classified 29 out of 30 teachers in each group. The Mahalanohis D-square, a measure of the distinctness of separation of the means of the two groups, was 8.8169, indicating a clear separation, with an F (6,53) of 20.1421, which is significant at $p < .001$. Discriminant function coefficients, values that will classify sample members into the two populations with minimal error, are shown in Table 2. The F-value (df 1,58) and significance for each variable when taken separately are also shown in Table 2.

Table 1

Mean Standard Scores on Flanders and Carkhuff Scales

| Measure | High Group | | Low Group | | Differences |
	Mean	SD	Mean	SD	Between Groups
Flanders					
Cat. 3	54.481537	12.25	45.518555	3.92	8.962982
Cat. 7	45.283279	5.03	54.715591	11.62	-9.432312
Cat. 9	55.600555	11.49	44.399857	3.13	11.200699
Carkhuff					
Scale E	57.876236	6.27	42.123596	6.27	15.752640
Scale C	56.969208	8.35	43.025238	6.05	13.943970
Scale PR	56.015900	8.00	43.983566	8.25	12.032333

Figure 1

Mean Standard Scores for High and Low Success Promotion
Groups on Flanders and Carkhuff Scales

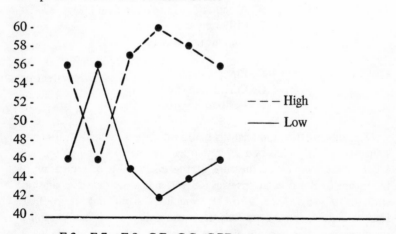

Categories on Flanders and Carkhuff Scales

Table 2

Discriminant Coefficients for Standard Scores on
Flanders and Carkhuff Scales

Variable	Coefficient	F-Value
F-3	561.30718	14.58*
F-7	-18.951071	16.59*
F-9	13.679045	26.50*
C-E	66.504925	94.76*
C-C	18.373460	54.84*
C-PR	13.791174	32.91*

*Significant at $p < .001$

Summary and Conclusions

The patterns which characterize a teacher who tends to promote the child's own goals involve using student's ideas, avoiding the use of criticism, providing a climate in which students feel free to initiate ideas, being aware of the meanings that a situation has for a student, being genuine in his responses, and showing positive regard for the student as a person. Each of the Carkhuff Scales, taken separately, is highly significant in discriminating high and low groups in success promotion, with empathy by itself contributing heavily to the discriminating power. While Category 9 on the Flanders' System of Interaction Analysis is a measure of student behavior rather than of teacher behavior, it illustrates well the fact that students respond to teachers' non-punitive use of their ideas. Not only do teachers in High and Low groups on Success Promotion perform differently, but their students behave in a discriminably different way.

When the success promotion scale is used alone, the score may serve as a guide to the probable presence of the qualities which have here been found to have strong relationships to this factor. Whether these qualities are components or correlates of success promotion is a subject for further study.

The measures used appear to discriminate quite effectively teachers in the criterion groups of high and low success promotion. While the

103

discriminating power may be less when used on unselected groups, it seems reasonable to expect that the approach used here will be useful to classify and evaluate teachers for in-service and pre-service training and to provide feedback for teachers who wish to increase their effectiveness.

1. Skinner, B. F. *The technology of teaching.* New York: Appleton-Century-Crofts, 1968. Pp. 57-58.

2. LaBenne, W. D. and Greene, B. I. *Educational implication of self-concept theory.* Pacific Palisades, California: Goodyear Publishing Co., 1968. P. 29.

3. Purkey, W. W. *Self-concept and school achievement.* Englewood Cliffs, N.J.: Prentice-Hall, 1970.

4. Neill, A. S. *Summerhill.* New York: Hart Publishing Co., 1960. P. 29.

5. Cronbach, L. J. *Educational psychology.* New York: Harcourt, Brace and World, 1963. P. 479.

6. Carkhuff, R. R. *Helping and human relations: A primer for lay and professional helpers. Vol. I. Selection and training. Vol. II. Practice and research.* New York: Holt, Rinehart and Winston, 1969.

7. Aspy, D. N. Better self-concepts through success. *Journal of Negro Education.* December, 1970.

8. Cooley, W. W. and Lohnes, P. R. *Multivariate procedures for the behavioral sciences.* New York: John Wiley and Sons, 1962. Pp. 116-33.

9. Fisher, R. A. and Yates, F. *Statistical tables for biological, agricultural and medical research.* 6th Ed. Edinburgh: Oliver and Boyd, Ltd., 1964.

Student Involvement: 8
IN HUMANE CLASSROOMS
STUDENTS GET EXCITED

Every classroom teacher is familiar with the impact of watching twenty-five or more students file into a room and of realizing the problems involved in creating a learning situation for them. The usual process grows from a disorganized, somewhat chaotic interaction, to some state of cooperative activity. Generally this entails getting the students' attention focused on a common point. Thus, "getting students' attention" may be described as one goal for classroom management, and is therefore of central concern to beginning teachers.

The importance of getting students' attention is well established by research into the relationship between attention and learning. Lahaderne reports, "a positive relationship was found between measures of students' attention and scores on achievement and intelligence tests."[1] Moore states that "one study showed that the poorer performance of retardates is due to their initial difficulty in directing attention."[2] Marsh found a -.58 correlation between achievement and student behavior indicating inattention.[3]

A more indirect measure of the relationship between learning and attention is found in Siegel's work.[4] In one study he reports that "it could be argued that readers are able to inhibit attention to (ignore) irrelevant stimuli more quickly (and thoroughly) than do the poorer readers." This position is supported by Samuels whose study indicated that "poor readers with no picture present learned more words (p. 201). Among better readers the difference was not as significant."[5]

Another aspect of attention is summarized by Crosby and Blatt in the following: "Surely the crucial point for education is that attention as stimulus selection is, at least within rather broad limits, a learned response and therefore susceptible to manipulation by the teacher."[6] Siegel and Corsini support this general thesis in this statement, "it appears that 8-year olds show little incidental learning, regardless of the nature of the incidental material, primarily because they fail to attend to the peripheral material unless instructed to do so."[7] Moore reports that for mental retardates "results indicated that pre-training facilitated word learning in retardates who had a MA of eight or higher."[8]

The research generally supports three basic assertions about attention:

1. The pupil's attention is related positively to his learning.
2. The pupil's inattention is related negatively to his learning.
3. Attention is a learned response and can be taught.

These findings indicate that teachers who are trying to "get their students' attention" are pursuing a goal which is important to the learning process.

If "attention getting" is a relevant aspect of teaching and learning, it seems important to initiate systematic procedures for investigating it.

Mostofsky[9] presents a rather comprehensive discussion of the definitions of terms involved in determining relationships between attention and learning. His views are summarized in the following statements:

A. The position adopted by the stimulus control interpretation of attention is that attention always accompanies stimulus control and is never observable in its absence.
B. Cognitive-perceptual description: Selectivity and integration of sensory information are offered as examples of such descriptions of attention.
C. The word attention connotes a process, a state, or a relationship involving a subject reacting with and to his environment.

Without belaboring this vital issue, it seems sufficient to say that attention has been treated by researchers and generalists as a process in which a person sorts through the stimuli which bombard him at a given moment and selects one or a few as focal points. We then say that he has directed his attention to those focal points. This is not a precise definition, but it has provided a working basis for some significant research.

The problem, after defining terms, is that of determining the relationship of the variable to other things. In this instance we are concerned with the relationship of attention to learning. The *Journal of Education* expresses the general view of teachers in the statement: "the educator—from classroom teacher to itinerant theoretician—has long accepted attention as an obvious and fundamental given."[10] That psychologists share this attitude with educators is reflected in Samuels' assertion that "psychologists have long been aware of the central role of attentional processes in learning."[11] Perhaps the "obviousness" of this relationship has been a "hang-up" in the sense that people have not devoted as much research effort to it as to many other aspects of classroom learning.

Lahaderne[12] tried to close the gap between assuming that attention is important to learning in a classroom situation and providing data which support that assumption. His instrument employed four levels of attention: (1) the pupil is attentive, (2) the pupil is inattentive, (3) uncertain, and (4) unobservable. The observers achieved reliabilities of 85 to 100% agreement. This certainly suggests that his procedure measures some classroom behavior rather consistently. However, the instrument fails to differentiate between students who are attending and those who are excited by the classroom activity. In this sense it reflects a major assumption of many teachers that "getting students' attention" is a goal. This is further reflected in his finding that one of the teachers' major functions was to preserve the classroom order .... "The students were coaxed and compelled to adhere to a code of conduct that supported the order of the classroom."

Keeping control or maintaining attention is not the goal for potent teachers. This contention is supported by Jackson and Belford.[13] In their study they found that twenty elementary teachers identified as outstanding by their principals and superintendents agreed that "teachers gauge the success of their teaching not so much by the scores their pupils attain on achievement tests as by the involvement pupils demonstrate during ongoing class activities." They further reported that "the desire to witness these most moving of all experiences, and possibly to have a hand in their occurrence, doubtlessly increases the attractiveness of troubled, 'lost,' unwanted children in the eyes of many teachers." The general picture of these superior teachers was that they trusted their own experience of the relative importance of events in their classrooms, and they expected more than mere ritual to occur.

If the potent teachers expect more than attention, then it behooves us to look carefully at this dimension of classroom interaction.

Jackson differentiates between attention and involvement in his beautiful and comprehensive book, *Life in Classrooms.*[14]

He says, "attention and involvement are not the same conditions, and the teacher would do well to keep this distinction in mind." He further discriminates between these two dimensions when he states, "Even though he might labor to control attention and though he may be forced to rely on signs of alertness as indicators of involvement, it is the latter condition, rather than the former, that he is seeking to cultivate." Apparently he considers attention a kind of transition point toward involvement.

Even this strong a stance may be ineffective in the enhancement of student involvement in the classroom if it is not translated into some kind of tangible procedures which can focus teachers' attention upon it. For this purpose we present in the following section a scale and procedures for using it.

Measuring Student Involvement

The following scale was devised for measuring student involvement.

Level 1

The student(s) is not involved in the classroom activity prescribed by the teacher.

Examples: (1) He expresses a strong dissatisfaction with the present activity.

(2) He makes a remark unrelated to present activity.

Level 2

The student(s) participates about half of the time in the activity prescribed by the teacher.

Examples: (1) He makes a response to the activity and follows it by one unrelated to it.

(2) He expresses mild dissatisfaction with the present activity.

Level 3

The student(s) participates in the class actively, but only within the prescribed rules.

Examples: (1) All his responses are related to the class activity, but he seems merely to be "going along with the game."

(2) He expresses neither satisfaction nor dissatisfaction with the activity.

Level 4

The student(s) participates enthusiastically in the class activity, but sticks pretty much to the rules established by the teacher.

Examples: (1) All his responses are related to the class activity, and he seems to enjoy it.

(2) He expresses mild satisfaction with the activity.

108

Level 5

The student(s) participates enthusiastically in the class activity and goes beyond the rules established by the teacher.

Examples: (1) All his responses are related to the class activity, and his enthusiasm is reflected in his exploration of new ideas stemming from it.

(2) He expresses strong satisfaction with the activity.

Uses of the Scale

Clarification of our perception of effective classrooms. This use of the scale is designed to help those of us who say that student involvement is important, but have done little to evaluate its impact in the classroom. Since the scale is effective when applied to audio or video tape recordings, we can compile a group of sample tapes which demonstrate different levels of student involvement and institute the following process:

1. Ask teachers, principals, etc., to rank the tapes of the classes in terms of best to worst on a five (5) point scale.
2. Teach these personnel to use the Student Involvement Scale.
3. Using the same tapes employed in Step 1, ask these personnel to rate them for student involvement.
4. Compare their ratings for best and worst classes with their ratings for student involvement.
5. Discuss the results either to deal with the discrepancies between the ratings or to support the similarities.

Investigation of the achievement of student involvement in our classes. The purpose of this use of the scale is to determine how effectively we translate our beliefs into practice. The following procedure is suggested:

1. Video or audio tape your normal classroom activity.
2. Rate your own tapes using the Student Involvement Scale.
3. When you are comfortable with the procedure, invite a few colleagues to rate your tapes to see if they agree with your interpretation.
4. Video or audio tape record your classes every two weeks to determine the continuing level of student involvement. The cues from tape recordings might provide earlier signals than normal classroom feedback about students' changes in involvement.

Determination of activities which seem to involve "problem" students. This use of the Student Involvement Scale is designed to identify activities which appear to involve the student who seems not to be involved in the classroom activities. The following procedure has been employed successfully:

1. Tape record your classroom a few times so that the novelty wears off.
2. Tape record your classroom so that you get an extended sample of the problem student's behavior. He should be tape recorded only when he is unaware that you are concentrating on him. (With video taping a long range focus allows the cameraman to rotate the camera slightly and still record the activity of the target student.)
3. Rate the target student's level of involvement and describe the classroom activity. This will produce a list of activities as well as a measure of the extent to which they involve him. (Hopefully, somewhere along the line some activity really "grabs" him.)

This same procedure can be employed with an entire class or with groups.

Since teachers' time is valuable, the ratings for the classroom may be completed by rating three four-minute segments of the tape. Usually the best results are obtained by abstracting one segment near the beginning of the class, one about the middle, and the third near the end. These supply a pattern of involvement.

Results of Research with the Student Involvement Scale
Two pieces of research with the Student Involvement Scale provide clues as to "where we are" in this dimension of the classroom.

1. The scale was applied by three raters to audio tape recordings of seventy-five different elementary classrooms with these results:
   a. Mean Rating = 2.9
   b. Standard Deviation = 0.3
   c. Range = 1.0 to 4.3
2. Seventeen first grade teachers who received five one-hour training sessions with the Student Involvement Scale raised their mean rating from 2.7 to 3.4. This suggests that the scales do communicate to teachers and that they are effective vehicles for enhancing this dimension of classroom interaction.

Summary

This chapter takes the position that student involvement is an important aspect of the classroom. It further holds that we are currently accomplishing control over students more than we are releasing their energies along creative lines.

As a partial remedy for this lack of student involvement, two suggestions are made. *First,* a scale for measuring student involvement is described, and *second,* three specific uses for the scale are outlined.

The general hope is that teachers will view student involvement as a significant dimension of the classroom and will move to enhance it. Certainly, our students think it is an important dimension, and their protests are focused rather heavily around the cry that they want school experiences which are more relevant. This adds up to a plea which has become a demand for more meaningful involvement.

Our general thesis is this . . . . In a society in which expressions like "getting involved" and "being turned on" are almost slogans for the young, it is not enough for the school merely to "get kids' attention." We must "turn them on" in our classrooms, or we're going to become anachronisms in their eyes. You see, the strange situation is that we, the older generation, have created a world in which survival is guaranteed for most people. Now, most of our youth want to see just how exciting life can be, and they're demanding that they get experiences which challenge them. *This means that they're pushing us to test the limits of our existence, which is strange to many of us because we have seldom thought of approaching life that way.* It may really be true that "a little child shall lead them." *Our children may, in fact, carry us to new, exciting ways of being which we have never known.* Our choice is to get on the move or watch the kids move out of our lives.

1. Lahaderne, H. M. Attitudinal and intellectual correlates of attention: A study of four sixth-grade classrooms. *Journal of Educational Psychology,* October, 1968, *59,* 320-4.

2. Moore, J. J. Application of an attention theory to retardate word learning. *Teachers College Journal,* November, 1963, *35,* 49-50.

3. Marsh, J. E., Development report–Systematic observation of instruction behavior. USAF: Personality Training Research Center Development 1956, No. AFPTRC TN 56-52.

4. Siegel, A. W. Variables affecting incidental learning in children. *Child Development,* December, 1967, *39,* 957-68.

5. Samuels, S. J. Attentional process in reading: The effect of pictures on the acquisition of reading responses. *Journal of Educational Psychology,* December, 1967, *58,* 337-42.

6. Crosby, G. and Blatt, B. Attention and mental retardation. *Journal of Education,* February, 1968, *150,* 67-81.

7. Siegel, A. W. and Corsini, J. A. Attentional differences in children's incidental learning. *Journal of Educational Psychology,* February, 1969, *60,* 65-70.

8. Moore, *op. cit.*

9. Mostofsky, D. I. Concept of attention in education. *Journal of Education,* February, 1968, *150,* 3-91.

10. Editorial introduction to Concept of attention in education. (D. I. Mostofsky) *Journal of Education,* February, 1968, *150,* 3-91.

11. Samuels, *op. cit.*

12. Lahaderne, *op cit.*

13. Jackson, P. W. and Belford, E. Educational objectives and the joys of teaching. *The School Review,* 1965, *73,* 267-291.

14. Jackson, P. W. *Life in classrooms.* New York: Holt, Rinehart and Winston, 1968. P. 111.

Putting It All Together: 9
THE BURTONSVILLE STORY

The remaining issue is whether these scales can be employed by a school in the improvement of its program. Fortunately, several schools have begun such an investigation, and by reporting the results for one of them, it is possible to delineate some relevant aspects of the procedure which is emerging.

The teachers at the Burtonsville Elementary School in Burtonsville, Maryland, audio tape recorded one hour of their normal classroom activity and forwarded those recordings to our College of Education where three trained raters evaluated them for each of the scales mentioned earlier. The results are listed in Tables 1 and 2.

These results along with those of previous studies were then forwarded to the teachers and principal at Burtonsville Elementary School. The previous studies were included to provide information about the relationship of the scale ratings to other components of the school, i.e., achievement test gains and attendance. Also, they indicated procedures which might be employed by the Burtonsville School.

The principal and faculty at Burtonsville Elementary School decided to use the data from the tape ratings to investigate three phases of their program:

1. The relationship of the levels of facilitative conditions to student achievement.
2. The relationship of the levels of the facilitative conditions to student attendance.
3. The variation in the levels of facilitative conditions between days of the week. That is, were they more constructive on Monday than on Friday.

In addition to these studies they began to investigate procedures they might employ within their own faculties to enhance their already

Table 1

Teacher	Flanders' Categories									
	1	2	3	4	5	6	7	8	9	10
A	0	3	2	29	8	16	0	37	0	3
B	0	5	2	29	3	16	3	31	1	7
C	0	3	3	16	3	16	4	36	12	3
D	0	1	0	18	13	10	2	45	0	11
E	0	3	7	18	12	11	0	23	19	7
F	0	8	4	37	1	12	1	30	1	5
G	0	0	3	25	0	5	0	36	27	3
H	0	1	12	14	8	14	3	42	0	5
I	0	0	1	36	1	8	0	49	2	3
J	0	0	4	28	7	4	0	42	5	11
K	0	0	2	7	3	6	3	70	6	1
L	0	0	10	5	5	1	0	13	65	0
M	0	5	3	24	2	9	1	49	0	5
N	0	0	1	8	4	0	0	33	41	0
O	0	1	5	31	17	11	0	29	0	4
P	0	0	3	5	0	0	0	77	12	2
Q	0	15	2	28	0	6	0	45	3	1
R	0	3	1	30	0	10	1	36	0	20

% of Hour in Each Category

high levels of human nourishment. This extension of the study meant audio tape recording more classes throughout the year to determine the stability of the levels of human facilitation.

These are just beginnings, but they represent the kind of effort which we think is both possible and practical at this point in time. Certainly, it gives these teachers an opportunity to come to grips with the issue of just how effectively they are implementing their belief that the human being is important in their classrooms. Additionally, these teachers represent the kind of courageous educators who are asking bold questions and are willing to put themselves on the line to find the answers.

Table 2

Teacher	Success Promotion	Student Involve.	Meaning	Genuine-ness	Respect
A	3.3	4.0	3.0	3.3	3.6
B	4.0	4.3	3.9	3.6	3.9
C	3.9	4.1	4.0	4.0	3.8
D	3.0	4.0	3.0	3.0	3.8
E	4.1	4.5	4.4	4.3	4.0
F	3.0	4.1	4.0	4.1	4.0
G	3.7	4.4	4.2	3.8	4.2
H	3.0	3.7	3.7	3.5	3.4
I	3.8	4.3	4.0	4.3	4.3
J	3.5	3.9	3.8	3.9	3.6
K	4.0	4.4	3.5	3.7	3.7
L	5.0	5.0	4.9	4.9	5.0
M	3.0	4.0	3.8	3.7	3.8
N	4.0	4.2	3.8	3.9	4.5
O	3.0	4.0	3.5	3.3	3.6
P	3.7	3.5	3.5	4.0	3.5
Q	3.5	4.0	3.9	4.0	3.5
R	3.3	3.8	3.9	4.4	3.5

Average Level Achieved During One Hour of Classroom Teaching. Each of the Scales Has Five Points with "1" Representing Low Levels and "5" Representing High Levels.

One final piece of information seems of utmost importance. Since two principals simultaneously expressed an interest in pursuing this type of study, it was possible to observe the "administrator effect" upon this process. From a previous study we had assessed these two administrators' levels of empathy, congruence, and positive regard during an interview with an undergraduate student. The Burtonsville principal performed well above the minimal facilitative levels described by Truax and Carkhuff, while the second principal was well below those levels. The foregoing writing describes the results obtained by the

Burtonsville principal; and, by way of contrast, the second principal reported that his teachers would be too threatened to participate in such a study. The results of this phase of this investigation suggest that the principal's level of interpersonal functioning may be a significant factor in determining his teachers' willingness to become involved in this kind of in-service training. Perhaps the ultimate proof of the Burtonsville principal's trusting relationship with his faculty lies in the fact that even though his teachers were given the option of identifying their tapes with either their names or a code number, all of them printed their names on their tapes. Apparently this principal was able to communicate his genuineness in a manner which helped his teachers perform in professionally courageous ways. *This* is the climate in which we can afford to ask *real* questions and get *real* answers.

A National Consortium: 10
AN INVITATION AND A CHALLENGE

There are hundreds of educators across our country who are humanizing education by relating constructively to the people in their local systems, but in many instances they are somewhat alone in their efforts. That is, they find themselves in a situation which places prime importance upon non-human things. In these situations it is not that people do not count, but rather that other things are more important. Specifically, money, schedules, and machines too frequently receive more attention than teachers, students, and other people involved in the program. When this occurs, the problem of humanizing education is one of re-ordering priorities. This discrimination is significant, because obstacles to the humanization of education do not turn on black and white issues. Therefore, since most people will agree that people are important, we tend to stop at this point and our efforts are absorbed and ineffective in terms of changed behavior. We thus need a thrust which pushes beyond words and alters our daily behaviors in a constructive direction. This challenge has been accepted by a group of educators, and they have devised a vehicle which unifies their efforts. It has been named "A National Consortium for Humanizing Education."

The Consortium is national is scope in that it includes school systems which reach literally from coast to coast. They are (1) Montgomery County, Maryland, (2) Volusia County, Florida, (3) Dade County, Florida, (4) Shawnee Mission, Kansas, (5) Waco Independent School District, Waco, Texas, (6) Hardin County, Kentucky, and (7) Chico Public Schools, Chico, California. How did these schools get involved? Well, they demonstrated an active interest in humanizing their schools and have vigorous, on-going programs directed toward that end. We have been drawn together by our mutual interests and efforts, and our friendships have developed easily and naturally.

The leaders in the local systems are "good men" who, in concert with other local people, have been effective in maintaining a humanizing focus in their schools. They are

1. Montgomery County, Maryland — Dr. James T. Kenney

2. Hardin County, Kentucky — Mrs. Elizabeth Tate

3. Volusia County, Florida — Mr. Julian Markham

4. Shawnee Mission, Kansas — Mr. Jeff Maddox and Mr. Dan Lewis

5. Waco Independent Schools, Waco, Texas — Mr. Ross Clark and Mr. Vernon Payne

6. Chico Public Schools, Chico, California — Dr. Charles Millis

These leaders possess a rare combination of strength, compassion, and intelligence, and are able to do the difficult task of resolving the seeming contradiction between being human and teaching children something. They accomplish both.

The Details of the Consortium

The members of the Consortium have studied classroom procedures through research, reading, and interaction, and they share some ideas about them. These include:

1. The most important aspect of human behavior is the perception of the person behaving. This means that, to be effective, education must be primarily concerned with the personal meanings of the learning situation to the students.

2. The most important aspect of being human is a person's positive perception of himself. In short, his education should contribute to the person's perception that he is able and worthwhile.

3. The most important component of a humane classroom is the climate created by the teacher. Specifically, the classroom should have a supply of meaningful learning experiences and the teacher should maintain facilitative levels of empathy (understanding), congruence (genuineness), and positive regard (valuing) toward her students.

4. Facilitative interpersonal functioning can be learned; and since new technologies for assessing and teaching it are emerging, it behooves

all of us as professional educators to engage in processes employing these new procedures.

5. Teachers cannot be expected to maintain humane classrooms unless they themselves are treated humanely. In this sense, all of us share the responsibility, and this includes administrators, supervisors, professors, and parents.

6. Activities directed toward humanizing education should be researched as thoroughly as other efforts in the field. The "mystical era" of humanizing education is over, and each aspect of the thrust can and should be investigated with the best procedures available.

7. Research and technology developed for the humanization of education should be disseminated through research journals, symposia, and on-the-job training experiences. That is, professional people from other systems should be invited to observe and participate in a locally developed program.

8. Since many of our current problems are human ones, humanizing education is not a frill. It is an important thrust which requires our best efforts. It should not displace our accomplishment of other aspects of education, but neither should it be subordinated to them.

The Cooperative Efforts

Many types of cooperative efforts are possible within the structure of our National Consortium. Some of them follow:

1. *Workshops* for Core Workers at which outstanding speakers are invited to share their ideas with us. Carl Rogers, Robert Carkhuff, and Edmund Amidon have already done this and several other prominent people are scheduled for future meetings. These sessions are limited to relatively small numbers of people (30 or less) so that optimal sharing can occur.

2. *Professional presentations* at professional organizations such as the Texas ASCD and the AERA meetings where the ideas and cooperative research can be shared with others. The members each present a portion of the program which focuses upon their special area of interest. These ideas have been presented to various educational groups in thirty-eight states and ten foreign countries.

3. *Cooperative publications* in professional journals such as *Educational Leadership, Journal of Educational Research* and the *Personnel and Guidance Journal.* For example, Dr. James T.

Kenney's school, Burtonsville Elementary School in Maryland, conducted a research project reported in Chapter 9 of this book and in the March, 1971 issue of *Educational Leadership*. He and his staff compiled the raw data which made it possible to disseminate it to larger groups. In a sense, they demonstrated that humane conditions *can* be effectively assessed in a practical situation.

4. *Cooperative research* through which the basic questions can be investigated and theoretical issues extended. Again, we can illustrate this with a project at Waco, Texas, in which several schools are cooperating to assess the effect of humane conditions upon a variety of school settings as well as on large samples of students who will be classified under a variety of rubrics.

5. *Workshops in local schools* at which a representative of the Consortium provides a variety of services as listed below:
   A. Presents ideas to groups.
   B. Trains key local personnel in the use of the scales, so they can serve as local consultants.
   C. Trains large groups of local personnel who use the scales at their discretion.
   D. Organizes, designs, and trains local personnel for the execution of a local study.
   E. Trains local personnel who commit themselves to a long range relationship with the Consortium. This usually consists of sending audio tape recordings (once a month) to the trained raters at Northeast Louisiana University where they are evaluated. Incidentally, these people often become our best local consultants and trainers for workshops in their areas.

These cooperative efforts allow us to learn from each other (which is a continuous process) and to share our resources with other people. Perhaps it should be made clear that our training programs have ranged from large groups (1,200 teachers in Arlington, Texas) to small ones of fifteen teachers. They have been successful as assessed by the trainees themselves. In fact, it is gratifying to know that in the largest meeting the trainees gave the workshop an average rating of 7.5 on a 9.0 scale! Apparently the group has developed a model that works.

Participation in the Consortium

There are currently over 200 school systems across the country which are using the services of the Consortium in some way. Hopefully, each system is finding how it can use those services most effectively. That is our goal. The Arlington, Texas program included 1,200 teachers, which fit their needs; but by way of illustrating the range of programs, it is rewarding to note that one of the most exciting programs is developing in Hardin County, Kentucky, where groups of thirty have participated in both training programs and evaluation procedures voluntarily. It is important to note that the local personnel were joined by the superintendent and a supervisor, Mrs. Elizabeth Tate, in the training programs. Past programs indicate that this is a necessary ingredient in effective training programs.

The purpose of the Consortium is that of bringing together the people in education who, first, believe that schools should provide constructive climates for students, and second, are ready to develop and implement programs to accomplish that goal. Each of these conditions is necessary for effective participation in the Consortium, because it is action oriented in the sense that it wants to go beyond words and to create effective programs.

Perhaps you are concerned about how you can become affiliated with such a group. If you fit the two criteria listed above, you have the necessary credentials to begin. The second step is to become involved with the Consortium by contacting one of the core people listed in this chapter. That is our invitation and our challenge.

Epilogue

This book has presented both a rationale for humane classrooms and specific processes for developing them. In each chapter a specific dimension of humane interpersonal relationships has been presented, and it has been followed by (1) a specific instrument for assessing the dimension, and (2) a study which both validated the dimension and illustrated how local investigators could employ it in their schools. It is hoped that this sequence of presentation will help to facilitate both the understanding of the dimensions and their use in a broad range of settings.

Finally, the book presented the central ideas and practices through which educators could work together toward creating a national thrust for the development of programs for humanizing classrooms. Essentially, this book is *all* about going beyond rhetoric to the most basic problems of creating learning situations which nourish the truly humane characteristics of learners so that we can help them grow constructively in the full sense of those words.

Aspy, David N.

Toward a technology for
humanizing education